Contents

Trial Memorandum Of The United States House Of Representatives In The Impeachment Trial Of President Donald J. Trump 1

Reply Memorandum Of The United States House Of Representatives In The Impeachment Trial Of President Donald J. Trump 115

United States House of Representatives

Adam B. Schiff
Jerrold Nadler
Zoe Lofgren
Hakeem S. Jeffries
Val Butler Demings
Jason Crow
Sylvia R. Garcia
U.S. House of Representatives Managers

IN THE SENATE OF THE UNITED STATES
Sitting as a Court of Impeachment

In re

**IMPEACHMENT OF
PRESIDENT DONALD J. TRUMP**

TRIAL MEMORANDUM
OF THE UNITED STATES HOUSE OF REPRESENTATIVES
IN THE IMPEACHMENT TRIAL OF PRESIDENT DONALD J. TRUMP

United States House of Representatives

Adam B. Schiff
Jerrold Nadler
Zoe Lofgren
Hakeem S. Jeffries
Val Butler Demings
Jason Crow
Sylvia R. Garcia

U.S. House of Representatives Managers

TABLE OF CONTENTS

INTRODUCTION 1

BACKGROUND 9

I.   CONSTITUTIONAL GROUNDS FOR PRESIDENTIAL IMPEACHMENT 9

II. THE HOUSE'S IMPEACHMENT OF PRESIDENT DONALD J. TRUMP AND PRESENTATION OF
     THIS MATTER TO THE SENATE 12

ARGUMENT 16

I.   THE SENATE SHOULD CONVICT PRESIDENT TRUMP OF ABUSE OF POWER 16

     A.   President Trump Exercised His Official Power to Pressure Ukraine into Aiding His
          Reelection 16

     B.   President Trump Exercised Official Power to Benefit Himself Personally 22

     C.   President Trump Jeopardized U.S. National Interests 28

II. THE SENATE SHOULD CONVICT PRESIDENT TRUMP OF OBSTRUCTION OF CONGRESS 30

     A.   The House Is Constitutionally Entitled to the Relevant Information in an
          Impeachment Inquiry 31

     B.   President Trump's Obstruction of the Impeachment Inquiry Violates Fundamental
          Constitutional Principles 34

     C.   President Trump's Excuses for His Obstruction Are Meritless 36

III. THE SENATE SHOULD IMMEDIATELY REMOVE PRESIDENT TRUMP FROM OFFICE TO
     PREVENT FURTHER ABUSES 41

     A.   President Trump's Repeated Abuse of Power Presents an Ongoing Threat to Our
          Elections 41

     B.   President Trump's Obstruction of Congress Threatens Our Constitutional Order 44

     C.   The Senate Should Convict and Remove President Trump to Protect Our System
          of Government and National Security Interests 45

ATTACHED STATEMENT OF MATERIAL FACTS .... SMF 1-61

INTRODUCTION

President Donald J. Trump used his official powers to pressure a foreign government to interfere in a United States election for his personal political gain, and then attempted to cover up his scheme by obstructing Congress's investigation into his misconduct. The Constitution provides a remedy when the President commits such serious abuses of his office: impeachment and removal. The Senate must use that remedy now to safeguard the 2020 U.S. election, protect our constitutional form of government, and eliminate the threat that the President poses to America's national security.

The House adopted two Articles of Impeachment against President Trump: the first for abuse of power, and the second for obstruction of Congress.[1] The evidence overwhelmingly establishes that he is guilty of both. The only remaining question is whether the members of the Senate will accept and carry out the responsibility placed on them by the Framers of our Constitution and their constitutional Oaths.

Abuse of Power

President Trump abused the power of his office by pressuring the government of Ukraine to interfere in the 2020 U.S. Presidential election for his own benefit. In order to pressure the recently elected Ukrainian President, Volodymyr Zelensky, to announce investigations that would advance President Trump's political interests and his 2020 reelection bid, the President exercised his official power to withhold from Ukraine critical U.S. government support—$391 million of vital military aid and a coveted White House meeting.[2]

---

[1] H. Res. 755, 116th Cong. (2019).
[2] *See* Statement of Material Facts (Statement of Facts) (Jan. 18, 2020), ¶¶ 1-151 (filed as an attachment to this Trial Memorandum).

During a July 25, 2019 phone call, after President Zelensky expressed gratitude to President Trump for American military assistance, President Trump immediately responded by asking President Zelensky to "do us a favor though."[3] The "favor" he sought was for Ukraine to publicly announce two investigations that President Trump believed would improve his domestic political prospects.[4] One investigation concerned former Vice President Joseph Biden, Jr.—a political rival in the upcoming 2020 election—and the false claim that, in seeking the removal of a corrupt Ukrainian prosecutor four years earlier, then-Vice President Biden had acted to protect a company where his son was a board member.[5] The second investigation concerned a debunked conspiracy theory that Russia did not interfere in the 2016 Presidential election to aid President Trump, but instead that Ukraine interfered in that election to aid President Trump's opponent, Hillary Clinton.[6]

These theories were baseless. There is no credible evidence to support the allegation that the former Vice President acted improperly in encouraging Ukraine to remove an incompetent and corrupt prosecutor in 2016.[7] And the U.S. Intelligence Community, the Senate Select Committee on Intelligence, and Special Counsel Robert S. Mueller, III unanimously determined that Russia, not Ukraine, interfered in the 2016 U.S. Presidential election "in sweeping and systematic fashion" to help President Trump's campaign.[8] In fact, the theory that Ukraine, rather than Russia, interfered in the 2016 election has been advanced by Russia's intelligence services as part of Russia's propaganda campaign.[9]

---

[3] *Id.* ¶¶ 75-76.
[4] *Id.* ¶¶ 76-77.
[5] *Id.* ¶¶ 11-12.
[6] *Id.* ¶¶ 11, 76.
[7] *Id.* ¶ 12.
[8] *Id.* ¶ 13.
[9] *Id.* ¶ 14.

Although these theories were groundless, President Trump sought a public announcement by Ukraine of investigations into them in order to help his 2020 reelection campaign.[10] An announcement of a Ukrainian investigation into one of his key political rivals would be enormously valuable to President Trump in his efforts to win reelection in 2020—just as the FBI's investigation into Hillary Clinton's emails had helped him in 2016. And an investigation suggesting that President Trump did not benefit from Russian interference in the 2016 election would give him a basis to assert—falsely—that he was the victim, rather than the beneficiary, of foreign meddling in the last election. Ukraine's announcement of that investigation would bolster the perceived legitimacy of his Presidency and, therefore, his political standing going into the 2020 race.

Overwhelming evidence shows that President Trump solicited these two investigations in order to obtain a personal political benefit, not because the investigations served the national interest.[11] The President's own National Security Advisor characterized the efforts to pressure Ukraine to announce investigations in exchange for official acts as a "drug deal."[12] His Acting Chief of Staff candidly confessed that President Trump's decision to withhold security assistance was tied to his desire for an investigation into alleged Ukrainian interference in the 2020 election, stated that there "is going to be political influence in foreign policy," and told the American people to "get over it."[13] Another one of President Trump's key national security advisors testified that the agents pursuing the President's bidding were "involved in a domestic political errand," not national security policy.[14] And, immediately after speaking to President Trump by phone about the investigations, one of President Trump's ambassadors involved in carrying out the President's agenda in Ukraine

---

[10] *See, e.g., id.* ¶ 53.
[11] *See, e.g., id.* ¶¶ 16, 18.
[12] *Id.* ¶ 59.
[13] *Id.* ¶¶ 120-21.
[14] *Id.* ¶ 122.

said that President Trump "did not give a [expletive] about Ukraine," and instead cared only about "big stuff" that benefitted him personally, like "the Biden investigation."[15]

To execute his scheme, President Trump assigned his personal attorney, Rudy Giuliani, the task of securing the Ukrainian investigations.[16] Mr. Giuliani repeatedly and publicly emphasized that he was *not* engaged in foreign policy but was instead seeking a personal benefit for his client, Donald Trump.[17]

President Trump used the vast powers of his office as President to pressure Ukraine into announcing these investigations. President Trump illegally withheld $391 million in taxpayer-funded military assistance to Ukraine that Congress had appropriated for expenditure in fiscal year 2019.[18] That assistance was a critical part of long-running bipartisan efforts to advance the security interests of the United States by ensuring that Ukraine is properly equipped to defend itself against Russian aggression.[19] Every relevant Executive Branch agency agreed that continued American support for Ukraine was in America's national security interests, but President Trump ignored that view and personally ordered the assistance held back, even after serious concerns—now confirmed by the Government Accountability Office (GAO)[20]—were raised within his Administration about the legality of withholding funding that Congress had already appropriated.[21] President Trump released the funding only after he got caught trying to use the security assistance as leverage to obtain foreign interference in his reelection campaign. When news of his scheme to withhold the funding broke,

---

[15] *Id.* ¶ 88.
[16] *See, e.g., id.* ¶ 24.
[17] *See, e.g., id.* ¶¶ 19, 25, 145-47.
[18] *Id.* ¶¶ 28-48.
[19] *Id.* ¶¶ 30-31.
[20] *Id.* ¶ 46.
[21] *Id.* ¶¶ 43, 46-48.

4

and shortly after investigative committees in the House opened an investigation, President Trump relented and released the aid.[22]

As part of the same pressure campaign, President Trump withheld a crucial White House meeting with President Zelensky—a meeting that he had previously promised and that was a shared goal of both the United States and Ukraine.[23] Such face-to-face Oval Office meetings with a U.S. President are immensely important for international credibility.[24] In this case, an Oval Office meeting with President Trump was critical to the newly elected Ukrainian President because it would signal to Russia—which had invaded Ukraine in 2014 and still occupied Ukrainian territory—that Ukraine could count on American support.[25] That meeting still has not occurred, even though President Trump has met with over a dozen world leaders at the White House since President Zelensky's election—including an Oval Office meeting with Russia's top diplomat.[26]

President Trump's solicitation of foreign interference in our elections to secure his own political success is precisely why the Framers of our Constitution provided Congress with the power to impeach a corrupt President and remove him from office. One of the Founding generation's principal fears was that foreign governments would seek to manipulate American elections—the defining feature of our self-government. Thomas Jefferson and John Adams warned of "foreign Interference, Intrigue, Influence" and predicted that, "as often as Elections happen, the danger of foreign Influence recurs."[27] The Framers therefore would have considered a President's attempt to corrupt America's democratic processes by demanding political favors from foreign powers to be a singularly pernicious act. They designed impeachment as the remedy for such misconduct because a

---

[22] *See, e.g., id.* ¶¶ 127, 131.
[23] *See id.* ¶¶ 49-69.
[24] *Id.* ¶ 50.
[25] *Id.* ¶¶ 3-4, 50.
[26] *See id.* ¶ 137.
[27] Letter from John Adams to Thomas Jefferson (Dec. 6, 1787) (Adams-Jefferson Letter), https://perma.cc/QWD8-222B.

President who manipulates U.S. elections to his advantage can avoid being held accountable by the voters through those same elections. And they would have viewed a President's efforts to encourage foreign election interference as all the more dangerous where, as here, those efforts are part of an ongoing pattern of misconduct for which the President is unrepentant.

The House of Representatives gathered overwhelming evidence of President Trump's misconduct, which is summarized in the attached Statement of Material Facts and in the comprehensive reports prepared by the House Permanent Select Committee on Intelligence and the Committee on the Judiciary.[28] On the strength of that evidence, the House approved the First Article of Impeachment against President Trump for abuse of power.[29] The Senate should now convict him on that Article. President Trump's continuing presence in office undermines the integrity of our democratic processes and endangers our national security.

Obstruction of Congress

President Trump obstructed Congress by undertaking an unprecedented campaign to prevent House Committees from investigating his misconduct. The Constitution entrusts the House with the "sole Power of Impeachment."[30] The Framers thus ensured what common sense requires—that the House, and not the President, determines the existence, scope, and procedures of an impeachment investigation into the President's conduct. The House cannot conduct such an investigation effectively if it cannot obtain information from the President or the Executive Branch about the Presidential misconduct it is investigating. Under our constitutional system of divided

---

[28] *See Impeachment of Donald J. Trump, President of the United States: Report of the Comm. on the Judiciary of the H. of Representatives, together with Dissenting Views, to Accompany H. Res. 755*, H. Rep. No. 116-346 (2019); *Report of the H. Permanent Select Comm. on Intelligence on the Trump-Ukraine Impeachment Inquiry, together with Minority Views*, H. Rep. No. 116-335 (2019); *see also* Majority Staff of the H. Comm. on the Judiciary, 116th Cong., *Constitutional Grounds for Presidential Impeachment* (Comm. Print 2019).

[29] H. Res. 755, at 2-5.

[30] U.S. Const., Art. I, § 2, cl. 5.

powers, a President cannot be permitted to hide his offenses from view by refusing to comply with a Congressional impeachment inquiry and ordering Executive Branch agencies to do the same. That conclusion is particularly important given the Department of Justice's position that the President cannot be indicted. If the President could both avoid accountability under the criminal laws and preclude an effective impeachment investigation, he would truly be above the law.

But that is what President Trump has attempted to do, and why President Trump's conduct is the Framers' worst nightmare. He directed his Administration to defy every subpoena issued in the House's impeachment investigation.[31] At his direction, the White House, Department of State, Department of Defense, Department of Energy, and Office of Management and Budget (OMB) refused to produce a single document in response to those subpoenas.[32] Several witnesses also followed President Trump's orders, defying requests for voluntary appearances and lawful subpoenas, and refusing to testify.[33] And President Trump's interference in the House's impeachment inquiry was not an isolated incident—it was consistent with his past efforts to obstruct the Special Counsel's investigation into Russian interference in the 2016 election.[34]

By categorically obstructing the House's impeachment inquiry, President Trump claimed the House's sole impeachment power for himself and sought to shield his misconduct from Congress and the American people. Although his sweeping cover-up effort ultimately failed—seventeen public officials courageously upheld their duty, testified, and provided documentary evidence of the President's wrongdoing[35]—his obstruction will do long-lasting and potentially irreparable damage to our constitutional system of divided powers if it goes unchecked.

---

[31] *See* Statement of Facts ¶¶ 164-69.
[32] *Id.* ¶¶ 179-83.
[33] *See, e.g., id.* ¶¶ 186-87.
[34] *See id.* ¶¶ 191-93.
[35] *Id.* ¶¶ 187-90.

Based on the overwhelming evidence of the President's misconduct in attempting to thwart the impeachment inquiry, the House approved the Second Article of Impeachment, for obstruction of Congress.[36] The Senate should now convict President Trump on that Article. If it does not, future Presidents will feel empowered to resist any investigation into their own wrongdoing, effectively nullifying Congress's power to exercise the Constitution's most important safeguard against Presidential misconduct. That outcome would not only embolden this President to continue seeking foreign interference in our elections but would telegraph to future Presidents that they are free to engage in serious misconduct without accountability or repercussions.

* * *

The Constitution entrusts Congress with the solemn task of impeaching and removing from office a President who engages in "Treason, Bribery, or other high Crimes and Misdemeanors."[37] The impeachment power is an essential check on the authority of the President, and Congress must exercise this power when the President places his personal and political interests above those of the Nation. President Trump has done exactly that. His misconduct challenges the fundamental principle that Americans should decide American elections, and that a divided system of government, in which no single branch operates without the check and balance of the others, preserves the liberty we all hold dear.

The country is watching to see how the Senate responds. History will judge each Senator's willingness to rise above partisan differences, view the facts honestly, and defend the Constitution. The outcome of these proceedings will determine whether generations to come will enjoy a safe and secure democracy in which the President is not a king, and in which no one, particularly the President, is above the law.

---

[36] *See id.* ¶ 178; H. Res. 755, at 5-8.
[37] U.S. Const., Art. II, § 4.

BACKGROUND

I.   CONSTITUTIONAL GROUNDS FOR PRESIDENTIAL IMPEACHMENT

To understand why President Trump must be removed from office now, it is necessary to understand why the Framers of our Constitution included the impeachment power as an essential part of the republic they created.

The Constitution entrusts Congress with the exclusive power to impeach the President and to convict and remove him from office. Article I vests the House with the "sole Power of Impeachment,"[38] and the Senate with the "sole Power to try all Impeachments" and to "convict[]" upon a vote of two thirds of its Members.[39] The Constitution specifies that the President "shall be removed from Office on Impeachment for, and Conviction of, Treason, Bribery, or other high Crimes and Misdemeanors."[40] The Constitution further provides that the Senate may vote to permanently "disqualif[y]" an impeached President from government service.[41]

The President takes an oath to "faithfully execute the Office of the President of the United States."[42] Impeachment imposes a check on a President who violates that oath by using the powers of the office to advance his own interests at the expense of the national interest. Fresh from their experience under British rule by a king, the Framers were concerned that corruption posed a grave threat to their new republic. As George Mason warned the other delegates to the Constitutional Convention, "if we do not provide against corruption, our government will soon be at an end."[43] The Framers stressed that a President who "act[s] from some corrupt motive or other" or "willfully

---

[38] U.S. Const., Art. I, § 2, cl. 5.
[39] U.S. Const., Art. I, § 3, cl. 6.
[40] U.S. Const., Art. II, § 4.
[41] U.S. Const., Art. I, § 3, cl. 6.
[42] U.S. Const., Art. II, § 1, cl. 8.
[43] 2 *The Records of the Federal Convention of 1787*, at 392 (Max Farrand ed.,1911) (Farrand).

abus[es] his trust" must be impeached,[44] because the President "will have great opportunitys of abusing his power."[45]

The Framers recognized that a President who abuses his power to manipulate the democratic process cannot properly be held accountable by means of the very elections that he has rigged to his advantage.[46] The Framers specifically feared a President who abused his office by sparing "no efforts or means whatever to get himself re-elected."[47] Mason asked: "Shall the man who has practised corruption & by that means procured his appointment in the first instance, be suffered to escape punishment, by repeating his guilt?"[48]

Thus, the Framers resolved to hold the President "impeachable whilst in office" as "an essential security for the good behaviour of the Executive."[49] By empowering Congress to immediately remove a President when his misconduct warrants it, the Framers established the people's elected representatives as the ultimate check on a President whose corruption threatened our democracy and the Nation's core interests.[50]

The Framers particularly feared that foreign influence could undermine our new system of self-government.[51] In his farewell address to the Nation, President George Washington warned Americans "to be constantly awake, since history and experience prove that foreign influence is one

---

[44] *Background and History of Impeachment: Hearing Before the Subcomm. on the Constitution of the H. Comm. on the Judiciary*, 105th Cong. 49 (1998) (quoting James Iredell).

[45] 2 Farrand at 67.

[46] *See id.* at 65.

[47] *Id.* at 64.

[48] *Id.* at 65.

[49] *Id.* at 64.

[50] *See The Federalist No. 65* (Alexander Hamilton).

[51] *See, e.g.*, 2 Farrand at 65-66; George Washington, Farewell Address (Sept. 19, 1796), *George Washington Papers, Series 2, Letterbooks 1754-1799: Letterbook 24, April 3, 1793–March 3, 1797*, Library of Congress (Washington Farewell Address); Adams-Jefferson Letter, https://perma.cc/QWD8-222B.

of the most baneful foes of republican government."[52] Alexander Hamilton cautioned that the

"most deadly adversaries of republican government" may come "chiefly from the desire in foreign

powers to gain an improper ascendant in our councils."[53] James Madison worried that a future

President could "betray his trust to foreign powers," which "might be fatal to the Republic."[54] And,

of particular relevance now, in their personal correspondence about "foreign Interference," Thomas

Jefferson and John Adams discussed their apprehension that "as often as Elections happen, the

danger of foreign Influence recurs."[55]

Guided by these concerns, the Framers included within the Constitution various

mechanisms to ensure the President's accountability and protect against foreign influence—

including a requirement that Presidents be natural-born citizens of the United States,[56] prohibitions

on the President's receipt of gifts, emoluments, or titles from foreign states,[57] prohibitions on

profiting from the Presidency,[58] and, of course, the requirement that the President face reelection

after a four-year Term.[59] But the Framers provided for impeachment as a final check on a President

who sought foreign interference to serve his personal interests, particularly to secure his own

reelection.

In drafting the Impeachment Clause, the Framers adopted a standard flexible enough to

reach the full range of potential Presidential misconduct: "Treason, Bribery, or other high Crimes

and Misdemeanors."[60] The decision to denote "Treason" and "Bribery" as impeachable conduct

---

[52] Washington Farewell Address.
[53] *The Federalist No. 68* (Alexander Hamilton).
[54] 2 Farrand at 66.
[55] Adams-Jefferson Letter, https://perma.cc/QWD8-222B.
[56] U.S. Const., Art. II, § 1, cl. 5.
[57] U.S. Const., Art. I, § 9, cl. 8.
[58] U.S. Const., Art. II, § 1, cl. 7.
[59] U.S. Const., Art. II, § 1, cl. 1.
[60] U.S. Const., Art. II, § 4; *see* 2 Farrand at 550.

reflects the Founding-era concerns over foreign influence and corruption. But the Framers also

recognized that "many great and dangerous offenses" could warrant impeachment and immediate

removal of a President from office.[61] These "other high Crimes and Misdemeanors" provided for

by the Constitution need not be indictable criminal offenses. Rather, as Hamilton explained,

impeachable offenses involve an "abuse or violation of some public trust" and are of "a nature

which may with peculiar propriety be denominated political, as they relate chiefly to injuries done

immediately to the society itself."[62] The Framers thus understood that "high crimes and

misdemeanors" would encompass acts committed by public officials that inflict severe harm on the

constitutional order.[63]

II. THE HOUSE'S IMPEACHMENT OF PRESIDENT DONALD J. TRUMP AND PRESENTATION OF THIS MATTER TO THE SENATE

Committees of the House have undertaken investigations into allegations of misconduct by

President Trump and his Administration. On September 9, 2019, after evidence surfaced that the

President and his associates were seeking Ukraine's assistance in the President's reelection, the

House Permanent Select Committee on Intelligence, together with the Committees on Oversight

and Reform and Foreign Affairs, announced a joint investigation into the President's conduct and

issued document requests to the White House and State Department.[64]

On September 24, 2019, Speaker Nancy Pelosi announced that the House was "moving

forward with an official impeachment inquiry" and directed the Committees to "proceed with their

investigations under that umbrella of [an] impeachment inquiry."[65] They subsequently issued

---

[61] 2 Farrand at 550.

[62] *The Federalist No. 65* (Alexander Hamilton) (capitalization altered).

[63] These issues are discussed at length in the report by the House Committee on the Judiciary. *See* H. Rep. No. 116-346, at 28-75.

[64] Statement of Facts ¶ 160.

[65] *Id.* ¶ 161.

12

multiple subpoenas for documents as well as requests and subpoenas for witness interviews and testimony.[66] On October 31, 2019, the House approved a resolution adopting procedures to govern the impeachment inquiry.[67]

Both before and after Speaker Pelosi's announcement, President Trump categorically refused to provide any information in response to the House's inquiry. He stated that "we're fighting all the subpoenas," and that "I have an Article II, where I have the right to do whatever I want as president."[68] Through his White House Counsel, the President later directed his Administration not to cooperate.[69] Heeding the President's directive, the Executive Branch did not produce any documents in response to subpoenas issued by the three investigating Committees,[70] and nine current or former Administration officials, including the President's top aides, continue to refuse to comply with subpoenas for testimony.[71]

Notwithstanding the President's attempted cover-up, seventeen current and former government officials courageously complied with their legal obligations and testified before the three investigating Committees in depositions or transcribed interviews that all Members of the Committees—as well as staff from the Majority and Minority—were permitted to attend.[72] Some witnesses produced documentary evidence in their possession. In late November 2019, twelve of these witnesses, including three requested by the Minority, testified in public hearings convened by the Intelligence Committee.[73]

---

[66] *See id.* ¶¶ 166, 180, 183, 189-90.
[67] *Id.* ¶ 162.
[68] *Id.* ¶ 164.
[69] *Id.* ¶¶ 164-69.
[70] *Id.* ¶ 183.
[71] *Id.* ¶ 187.
[72] *Id.* ¶¶ 188-89.
[73] *Id.* ¶ 189.

Stressing the "overwhelming" evidence of misconduct already uncovered by the investigation, on December 3, 2019, the Intelligence Committee released a detailed nearly 300-page report documenting its findings, which it transmitted to the Judiciary Committee.[74] The Judiciary Committee held public hearings evaluating the constitutional standard for impeachment and the evidence against President Trump—in which the President's counsel was invited, but declined, to participate—and then reported two Articles of Impeachment to the House.[75]

On December 18, 2019, the House voted to impeach President Trump and adopted two Articles of Impeachment.[76] The First Article for Abuse of Power states that President Trump "abused the powers of the Presidency" by "soliciting the Government of Ukraine to publicly announce investigations that would benefit his reelection, harm the election prospects of a political opponent, and influence the 2020 United States Presidential election to his advantage."[77] President Trump sought to "pressure the Government of Ukraine to take these steps by conditioning official United States Government acts of significant value to Ukraine on its public announcement of the investigations."[78] President Trump undertook these acts "for corrupt purposes in pursuit of personal political benefit"[79] and "used the powers of the Presidency in a manner that compromised the national security of the United States and undermined the integrity of the United States democratic process."[80] These actions were "consistent" with President Trump's "previous invitations of foreign interference in United States elections,"[81] and demonstrated that President

---

[74] *Id.* ¶ 176; *see also* H. Rep. No. 116-335.
[75] Statement of Facts ¶ 176; *see also* H. Res. 755.
[76] Statement of Facts ¶ 178; H. Res. 755.
[77] H. Res. 755, at 2-3.
[78] *Id.*
[79] *Id.* at 3.
[80] *Id.*
[81] *Id.* at 4.

Trump "will remain a threat to national security and the Constitution if allowed to remain in office."[82]

The Second Article for Obstruction of Congress states that President Trump "abused the powers of the Presidency in a manner offensive to, and subversive of, the Constitution" when he "directed the unprecedented, categorical, and indiscriminate defiance of subpoenas issued by the House of Representatives pursuant to its 'sole Power of Impeachment.'"[83] Without "lawful cause or excuse, President Trump directed Executive Branch agencies, offices, and officials not to comply with those subpoenas" and "thus interposed the powers of the Presidency against the lawful subpoenas of the House of Representatives, and assumed to himself functions and judgments necessary to the exercise of the 'sole Power of Impeachment' vested by the Constitution in the House of Representatives."[84] The President's "complete defiance of an impeachment inquiry . . . served to cover up the President's own repeated misconduct and to seize and control the power of impeachment."[85] President Trump's misconduct was "consistent" with his "previous efforts to undermine United States Government investigations into foreign interference in United States elections,"[86] demonstrated that he has "acted in a manner grossly incompatible with self-governance," and established that he "will remain a threat to the Constitution if allowed to remain in office."[87]

---

[82] *Id.* at 5.
[83] *Id.* at 6.
[84] *Id.*
[85] *Id.* at 8.
[86] *Id.* at 7.
[87] *Id.* at 5, 8.

ARGUMENT

I. THE SENATE SHOULD CONVICT PRESIDENT TRUMP OF ABUSE OF POWER

President Trump abused the power of the Presidency by pressuring a foreign government to interfere in an American election on his behalf.[88] He solicited this foreign interference to advance his reelection prospects at the expense of America's national security and the security of Ukraine, a vulnerable American ally at war with Russia, an American adversary.[89] His effort to gain a personal political benefit by encouraging a foreign government to undermine America's democratic process strikes at the core of misconduct that the Framers designed impeachment to protect against. President Trump's abuse of power requires his conviction and removal from office.

An officer abuses his power if he exercises his official power to obtain an improper personal benefit while ignoring or undermining the national interest.[90] An abuse that involves an effort to solicit foreign interference in an American election is uniquely dangerous. President Trump's misconduct is an impeachable abuse of power.[91]

A. President Trump Exercised His Official Power to Pressure Ukraine into Aiding His Reelection

After President Zelensky won a landslide victory in Ukraine in April 2019, President Trump pressured the new Ukrainian President to help him win his own reelection by announcing investigations that were politically favorable for President Trump and designed to harm his political rival.[92]

---

[88] *See* Statement of Facts ¶¶ 1-157.

[89] *See id.* ¶¶ 1-157.

[90] *See, e.g., Report of the Impeachment Trial Comm. on the Articles Against Judge G. Thomas Porteous, Jr.*, S. Rep. No. 111-347, at 6-7 (2010); *Impeachment of Judge Alcee L. Hastings: Report of the H. Comm. of the Judiciary to Accompany H. Res. 499*, H. Rep. No. 100-810, at 1-5, 8, 41 (1988); 132 Cong. Rec. H4710-22 (daily ed. July 22, 1986) (impeachment of Judge Claiborne).

[91] For a more detailed discussion of abuse of power as an impeachable offense, see H. Rep. No. 116-346, at 43-48, 68-70, 78-81.

[92] Statement of Facts ¶¶ 1-151.

16

First, President Trump sought to pressure President Zelensky publicly to announce an investigation into former Vice President Biden and a Ukrainian gas company, Burisma Holdings, on whose board Biden's son sat.[93] As Vice President, Biden had in late 2015 encouraged the government of Ukraine to remove a Ukrainian prosecutor general who had failed to combat corruption.[94] The Ukrainian parliament removed the prosecutor in March 2016.[95] President Trump and his allies have asserted that the former Vice President acted in order to stop an investigation of Burisma and thereby protect his son.[96] This is false. There is no evidence that Vice President Biden acted improperly.[97] He was carrying out official United States policy—with the backing of the international community and bipartisan support in Congress—when he sought the removal of the prosecutor, who was himself corrupt.[98] In addition, the prosecutor's removal made it *more likely* that the investigation into Burisma would be pursued.[99] President Trump nevertheless sought an official Ukrainian announcement of an investigation into this theory.[100]

Second, President Trump sought to pressure President Zelensky publicly to announce an investigation into a conspiracy theory that Ukraine had colluded with the Democratic National Committee to interfere in the 2016 U.S. Presidential election in order to help the campaign of Hillary Clinton against then-candidate Donald Trump.[101] This theory was not only pure fiction, but malign Russian propaganda.[102] In the words of one of President Trump's own top National Security Council officials, President Trump's theory of Ukrainian election interference is "a fictional narrative

---

[93] *Id.* ¶¶ 11-12.
[94] *See id.* ¶ 12.
[95] *Id.*
[96] *Id.* ¶¶ 11, 17.
[97] *Id.* ¶ 12.
[98] *Id.*
[99] *Id.*
[100] *Id.*; *see also id.* ¶¶ 83-84, 150.
[101] *Id.* ¶¶ 11, 84.
[102] *Id.* ¶¶ 12-14.

17

that is being perpetrated and propagated by the Russian security services themselves" to deflect from Russia's culpability and to drive a wedge between the United States and Ukraine.[103] President Trump's own FBI Director confirmed that American law enforcement has "no information that indicates that Ukraine interfered with the 2016 presidential election."[104] The Senate Select Committee on Intelligence similarly concluded that Russia, not Ukraine, interfered in the 2016 U.S. Presidential election.[105] President Trump nevertheless seized on the false theory and sought an announcement of an investigation that would give him a basis to assert that Ukraine rather than Russia interfered in the 2016 election. Such an investigation would eliminate a perceived threat to his own legitimacy and boost his political standing in advance of the 2020 election.[106]

In furtherance of the corrupt scheme, President Trump exercised his official power to remove a perceived obstacle to Ukraine's pursuit of the two sham investigations. On April 24, 2019—one day after the media reported that former Vice President Biden would formally enter the 2020 U.S. Presidential race[107]—the State Department executed President Trump's order to recall the U.S. ambassador to Ukraine, a well-regarded career diplomat and anti-corruption crusader.[108] President Trump needed her "out of the way" because "she was going to make the investigations difficult for everybody."[109] President Trump then proceeded to exercise his official power to pressure Ukraine into announcing his desired investigations by withholding valuable support that Ukraine desperately needed and that he could leverage only by virtue of his office: $391 million in security assistance and a White House meeting.

---

[103] *Id.* ¶ 14.
[104] *Id.* ¶ 13.
[105] *Id.*
[106] *See id.* ¶¶ 11-13, 83-84.
[107] *Id.* ¶ 6.
[108] *Id.* ¶¶ 7-9.
[109] *Id.* ¶ 10 (quoting Mr. Giuliani).

President Trump illegally ordered the Office of Management and Budget to withhold $391 million in taxpayer-funded military and other security assistance to Ukraine.[110] This assistance would provide Ukraine with sniper rifles, rocket-propelled grenade launchers, counter-artillery radars, electronic warfare detection and secure communications, and night vision equipment, among other military equipment, to defend itself against Russian forces that occupied part of eastern Ukraine since 2014.[111] The new and vulnerable government headed by President Zelensky urgently needed this assistance—both because the funding itself was critically important to defend against Russia, and because the funding was a highly visible sign of American support for President Zelensky in his efforts to negotiate an end to the conflict from a position of strength.[112]

Every relevant Executive Branch agency supported the assistance, which also had broad bipartisan support in Congress.[113] President Trump, however, personally ordered OMB to withhold the assistance after the bulk of it had been appropriated by Congress and all of the Congressionally mandated conditions on assistance—including anti-corruption reforms—had been met.[114] The Government Accountability Office has determined that the President's hold was illegal and violated the Impoundment Control Act, which limits the President's authority to withhold funds that Congress has appropriated.[115]

---

[110] *Id.* ¶¶ 28-48.

[111] *Id.* ¶ 35.

[112] *See id.* ¶¶ 30-31, 34-35.

[113] *Id.* ¶ 39.

[114] *Id.* ¶¶ 39, 41-42.

[115] *Id.* ¶ 46. The GAO opinion addresses only the portion of the funds appropriated to the Department of Defense. The opinion explains that OMB and the State Department have not provided the information GAO needs to evaluate the legality of the hold placed by the President on the remaining funds.

The evidence is clear that President Trump conditioned release of the vital military assistance on Ukraine's announcement of the sham investigations. During a telephone conversation between the two Presidents on July 25, immediately after President Zelensky raised the issue of U.S. military support for Ukraine, President Trump replied: "I would like you to do us a favor though."[116] President Trump then explained that the "favor" he wanted President Zelensky to perform was to begin the investigations, and President Zelensky confirmed his understanding that the investigations should be done "openly."[117] In describing whom he wanted Ukraine to investigate, President Trump mentioned only two people: former Vice President Biden and his son.[118] And in describing the claim of foreign interference in the 2016 election, President Trump declared that "they say a lot of it started with Ukraine," and that "[w]hatever you can do, it's very important that you do it if that's possible."[119] Absent from the discussion was any mention by President Trump of anti-corruption reforms in Ukraine.

One of President Trump's chief agents for carrying out the President's agenda in Ukraine, Ambassador Gordon Sondland, testified that President Trump's effort to condition release of the much-needed security assistance on an announcement of the investigations was as clear as "two plus two equals four."[120] Sondland communicated to President Zelensky's advisor that Ukraine would likely not receive assistance unless President Zelensky publicly announced the investigations.[121] And President Trump later confirmed to Ambassador Sondland that President Zelensky "must announce the opening of the investigations and he should want to do it."[122]

---

[116] *Id.* ¶ 76.
[117] *Id.* ¶¶ 76, 80.
[118] *Id.* ¶ 82.
[119] *Id.* ¶ 77.
[120] *Id.* ¶ 101.
[121] *Id.* ¶ 110.
[122] *Id.* ¶ 114.

20

President Trump ultimately released the military assistance, but only after the press publicly reported the hold, after the President learned that a whistleblower within the Intelligence Community had filed a complaint about his misconduct, and after the House publicly announced an investigation of the President's scheme. In short, President Trump released the security assistance for Ukraine only after he got caught.[123]

Withheld White House Meeting

On April 21, 2019, the day President Zelensky was elected, President Trump invited him to a meeting at the White House.[124] The meeting would have signaled American support for the new Ukrainian administration, its strong anti-corruption reform agenda, and its efforts to defend against Russian aggression and to make peace.[125] President Trump, however, exercised his official power to withhold the meeting as leverage in his scheme to pressure President Zelensky into announcing the investigations to help his reelection campaign.

The evidence is unambiguous that President Trump and his agents conditioned the White House meeting on Ukraine's announcement of the investigations. Ambassador Sondland testified that President Trump wanted "a public statement from President Zelensky" committing to the investigations as a "prerequisite[]" for the White House meeting.[126] Ambassador Sondland further testified: "I know that members of this committee frequently frame these complicated issues in the form of a simple question: Was there a quid pro quo? As I testified previously with regard to the requested White House call and the White House meeting, the answer is yes."[127]

---

[123] *Id.* ¶¶ 103, 130-31.
[124] *Id.* ¶ 3.
[125] *See, e.g., id.* ¶ 4.
[126] *Id.* ¶ 88.
[127] *Id.* ¶ 52.

To this day, President Trump maintains leverage over President Zelensky. A White House meeting has still not taken place,[128] and President Trump continues publicly to urge Ukraine to conduct these investigations.[129]

B. President Trump Exercised Official Power to Benefit Himself Personally

Overwhelming evidence demonstrates that the announcement of investigations on which President Trump conditioned the official acts had no legitimate policy rationale, and instead were corruptly intended to assist his 2020 reelection campaign.[130]

First, although there was no basis for the two conspiracy theories that President Trump advanced,[131] public announcements that these theories were being investigated would be of immense political value to him—and him alone. The public announcement of an investigation of former Vice President Biden would yield enormous political benefits for President Trump, who viewed the former Vice President as a serious political rival in the 2020 U.S. Presidential election. Unsurprisingly, President Trump's efforts to advance the conspiracy theory accelerated after news broke that Vice President Biden would run for President in 2020.[132] President Trump benefited from such an announcement of a criminal investigation into his Presidential opponent in 2016.[133] An announcement of a criminal investigation regarding a 2020 rival would likewise be extremely helpful to his reelection prospects.

President Trump would similarly have viewed an investigation into Ukrainian interference in the 2016 election as helpful in undermining the conclusion that he had benefitted from Russian election interference in 2016, and that he was the preferred candidate of President Putin—both of

---

[128] *Id.* ¶ 137.

[129] *Id.* ¶¶ 141-42, 150.

[130] *See generally* Statement of Facts; H. Rep. No. 116-346; H. Rep. No. 116-335.

[131] Statement of Facts ¶¶ 11-15.

[132] *Id.* ¶¶ 16-19.

[133] *See id.* ¶¶ 154-56 (then-candidate Trump's actions relating to the FBI's investigation into Hillary Clinton).

which President Trump viewed as calling into question the legitimacy of his Presidency. An announcement that Ukraine was investigating its own alleged 2016 election interference would have turned these facts on their head. President Trump would have grounds to claim—falsely—that he was elected President in 2016 not because he was the beneficiary of Russian election interference, but *in spite of* Ukrainian election interference aimed at helping his opponent.

Second, agents and associates of President Trump who helped carry out his agenda in Ukraine confirmed that his efforts to pressure President Zelensky into announcing the desired investigations were intended for his personal political benefit rather than for a legitimate policy purpose. For example, after speaking with President Trump, Ambassador Sondland told a colleague that President Trump "did not give a [expletive] about Ukraine," and instead cared only about "big stuff" that benefitted him personally "like the Biden investigation that Mr. Giuliani was pushing."[134] And Mick Mulvaney, President Trump's Acting Chief of Staff, acknowledged to a reporter that there was a quid pro quo with Ukraine involving the military aid, conceded that "[t]here is going to be political influence in foreign policy," and stated, "I have news for everybody: get over it."[135]

Third, the involvement of President Trump's personal attorney, Mr. Giuliani—who has professional obligations to the President but not the Nation—underscores that President Trump sought the investigations for personal and political reasons rather than legitimate foreign policy reasons. Mr. Giuliani openly and repeatedly acknowledged that he was pursuing the Ukrainian investigations to advance the President's interests, stating: "this isn't foreign policy."[136] Instead, Mr.

---

[134] *Id.* ¶ 88.

[135] *Id.* ¶ 121. Mr. Mulvaney, along with his deputy Robert Blair and OMB official Michael Duffey—who were subpoenaed by the House, but refused to testify at the President's direction, *see id.* ¶ 187—would provide additional firsthand testimony regarding the President's withholding of official acts in exchange for Ukraine's assistance with his reelection.

[136] *Id.* ¶ 18.

23

Giuliani said that he was seeking information that "will be very, very helpful to my client."[137] Mr. Giuliani made similar representations to the Ukrainian government. In a letter to President-elect Zelensky, Mr. Giuliani stated that he "represent[ed] him [President Trump] *as a private citizen*, not as President of the United States" and was acting with the President's "knowledge and consent."[138] President Trump placed Mr. Giuliani at the hub of the pressure campaign on Ukraine, and directed U.S. officials responsible for Ukraine to "talk to Rudy."[139] Indeed, during their July 25 call, President Trump pressed President Zelensky to speak with Mr. Giuliani directly, stating: "Rudy very much knows what's happening and he is a very capable guy. If you could speak to him that would be great."[140]

Fourth, President Trump's pursuit of the sham investigations marked a dramatic deviation from longstanding bipartisan American foreign policy goals in Ukraine. Legitimate investigations could have been recognized as an anti-corruption foreign policy goal, but there was no factual basis for an investigation into the Bidens or into supposed Ukrainian interference in the 2016 election.[141] To the contrary, the requested investigations were precisely the type of political investigations that American foreign policy dissuades other countries from undertaking. That explains why the scheme to obtain the announcements was pursued through the President's chosen political appointees and his personal attorney;[142] why Trump Administration officials attempted to keep the scheme from becoming public due to its "sensitive nature";[143] why no credible explanation for the hold on security assistance was provided even within the U.S. government;[144] why, over Defense Department

---

[137] *Id.*
[138] *Id.* ¶ 19 (emphasis added).
[139] *Id.* ¶ 24.
[140] *Id.* ¶ 78.
[141] *Id.* ¶¶ 11-15, 122.
[142] *Id.*
[143] *Id.* ¶ 42.
[144] *Id.* ¶¶ 43-48.

24

objections, President Trump and his allies violated the law by withholding the aid;[145] and why, after the scheme was uncovered, President Trump falsely claimed that his pursuit of the investigations did not involve a quid pro quo.[146]

Fifth, American and Ukrainian officials alike saw President Trump's scheme for what it was: improper and political. As we expect the testimony of Ambassador John Bolton would confirm, President Trump's National Security Advisor stated that he wanted no "part of whatever drug deal" President Trump's agents were pursuing in Ukraine.[147] Dr. Hill testified that Ambassador Sondland was becoming involved in a "domestic political errand" in pressing Ukraine to announce the investigations.[148] Jennifer Williams, an advisor to Vice President Mike Pence, testified that the President's solicitation of investigations was a "domestic political matter."[149] Lt. Col. Alexander Vindman, the NSC's Director for Ukraine, testified that "[i]t is improper for the President of the United States to demand a foreign government investigate a U.S. citizen and a political opponent."[150] William Taylor, who took over as Chargé d'Affaires in Kyiv after President Trump recalled Ambassador Yovanovitch, emphasized that "I think it's crazy to withhold security assistance for help with a political campaign."[151] And George Kent, a State Department official, testified that "asking another country to investigate a prosecution for political reasons undermines our advocacy of the rule of law."[152]

---

[145] *Id.* ¶¶ 45-46.

[146] *Id.* ¶ 140.

[147] *Id.* ¶ 59. Although Bolton has not cooperated with the House's inquiry, he has offered to testify to the Senate if subpoenaed.

[148] *Id.* ¶ 58.

[149] *Id.* ¶ 84.

[150] *Id.* ¶ 83.

[151] *Id.* ¶ 118.

[152] *Id.* ¶ 55 (recalling his statement to Ambassador Volker in July 2019).

Ukrainian officials also understood that President Trump's corrupt effort to solicit the sham investigations would drag them into domestic U.S. politics. In response to the President's efforts, a senior Ukrainian official conveyed to Ambassador Taylor that President Zelensky "did not want to be used as a pawn in a U.S. reelection campaign."[153] Another Ukrainian official later stated that "it's critically important for the west not to pull us into some conflicts between their ruling elites[.]"[154] And when Ambassador Kurt Volker tried to warn President Zelensky's advisor against investigating President Zelensky's former political opponent—the prior Ukrainian president—the advisor retorted, "What, you mean like asking us to investigate Clinton and Biden?"[155] David Holmes, a career diplomat at the U.S. Embassy in Kyiv, highlighted this hypocrisy: "While we had advised our Ukrainian counterparts to voice a commitment to following the rule of law and generally investigating credible corruption allegations," U.S. officials were making "a demand that President Zelensky personally commit on a cable news channel to a specific investigation of President Trump's political rival."[156]

Finally, there is no credible alternative explanation for President Trump's conduct. It is not credible that President Trump sought announcements of the investigations because he was in fact concerned with corruption in Ukraine or burden-sharing with our European allies, as he claimed after the scheme was uncovered.[157]

Before news of former Vice President Biden's candidacy broke, President Trump showed no interest in corruption in Ukraine, and in prior years he approved military assistance to Ukraine without controversy.[158] After his candidacy was announced, President Trump remained indifferent

---

[153] *Id.* ¶ 68.
[154] *Id.* ¶ 104.
[155] *Id.* ¶ 150.
[156] *Id.* ¶ 151.
[157] *Id.* ¶ 143.
[158] *See id.* ¶¶ 2, 33.

26

to anti-corruption measures beyond the two investigations he was demanding.[159] When he first spoke with President Zelensky on April 21, President Trump ignored the recommendation of his national security advisors and did not mention corruption at all—even though the purpose of the call was to congratulate President Zelensky on a victory based on an anti-corruption platform.[160] President Trump's entire policy team agreed that President Zelensky was genuinely committed to reforms, yet President Trump refused a White House meeting that the team advised would support President Zelensky's anti-corruption agenda.[161] President Trump's own Department of Defense, in consultation with the State Department, had certified in May 2019 that Ukraine satisfied all anti-corruption standards needed to receive the Congressionally appropriated military aid, yet President Trump nevertheless withheld that vital assistance.[162] He recalled without explanation Ambassador Yovanovitch, who was widely recognized as a champion in fighting corruption,[163] disparaged her while praising a corrupt Ukrainian prosecutor general,[164] and oversaw efforts to cut foreign programs tasked with combating corruption in Ukraine and elsewhere.[165]

Moreover, had President Trump truly sought to assist Ukraine's anti-corruption efforts, he would have focused on ensuring that Ukraine actually *conducted* investigations of the purported issues he identified. But actual investigations were never the point. President Trump was interested only in the *announcement* of the investigations because that announcement would accomplish his real goal—bolstering his reelection efforts.[166]

---

[159] *See id.* ¶ 88.
[160] *See id.* ¶¶ 1-2.
[161] *See id.* ¶¶ 22-24.
[162] *See id.* ¶¶ 36 n.73, 39.
[163] *See id.* ¶ 7.
[164] *See id.* ¶¶ 8-9, 81.
[165] *See id.* ¶ 82 n.138.
[166] *See e.g., id.* ¶¶ 82, 131.

President Trump's purported concern about sharing the burden of assistance to Ukraine with Europe is equally without basis. From the time OMB announced the illegal hold until it was lifted, no credible reason was provided to Executive Branch agencies for the hold, despite repeated efforts by national security officials to obtain an explanation.[167] It was not until September—approximately two months after President Trump had directed the hold and after the President had learned of the whistleblower complaint—that the hold, for the first time, was attributed to the President's concern about other countries not contributing more to Ukraine.[168] If the President was genuinely concerned about burden-sharing, it makes no sense that he kept his own Administration in the dark about the issue for months, never made any contemporaneous public statements about it, never ordered a review of burden-sharing,[169] never ordered his officials to push Europe to increase their contributions,[170] and then released the aid without any change in Europe's contribution.[171] The concern about burden-sharing is an after-the-fact rationalization designed to conceal President Trump's abuse of power.

C.   President Trump Jeopardized U.S. National Interests

President Trump's efforts to solicit foreign interference to help his reelection campaign is pernicious, but his conduct is all the more alarming because it endangered U.S. national security, jeopardized our alliances, and undermined our efforts to promote the rule of law globally.

Ukraine is a "strategic partner of the United States" on the front lines of an ongoing conflict with Russia.[172] The United States has approved military assistance to Ukraine with bipartisan support since 2014, and that assistance is critical to preventing Russia's expansion and aggression.

---

[167] *See id.* ¶¶ 41-48.
[168] *See id.* ¶¶ 43-45.
[169] *See id.* ¶ 44.
[170] *See id.*
[171] *See id.* ¶ 131.
[172] *Id.* ¶ 28.

This military assistance—which President Trump withheld in service of his own political interests—"saves lives" by making Ukrainian resistance to Russia more effective.[173] It likewise advances American national security interests because, "[i]f Russia prevails and Ukraine falls to Russian dominion, we can expect to see other attempts by Russia to expand its territory and influence."[174] Indeed, the reason the United States provides assistance to the Ukrainian military is "so that they can fight Russia over there, and we don't have to fight Russia here."[175] President Trump's delay in providing the military assistance jeopardized these national security interests and emboldened Russia even though the funding was ultimately released—particularly because the delay occurred "when Russia was watching closely to gauge the level of American support for the Ukrainian Government."[176] But for a subsequent act of Congress, approximately $35 million of military assistance to Ukraine would have lapsed and been unavailable as a result of the President's abuse of power.[177]

The White House meeting that President Trump promised President Zelensky—but continues to withhold—would similarly have signaled to Russia that the United States stands behind Ukraine, showing "U.S. support at the highest levels."[178] By refusing to hold this meeting, President Trump denied Ukraine a showing of strength that could deter further Russian aggression and help Ukraine negotiate a favorable end to its war with Russia.[179] The withheld meeting also undercuts President Zelensky's domestic standing, diminishing his ability to advance his ambitious anti-corruption reforms.[180]

---

[173] *Id.* ¶ 31.
[174] *Id.*
[175] *Id.*
[176] *Id.* ¶ 4.
[177] *Id.* ¶¶ 132-33.
[178] *Id.* ¶ 4 & n.8.
[179] *See id.* ¶ 50.
[180] *See id.*

Equally troubling is that President Trump's scheme sent a clear message to our allies that the United States may capriciously withhold critical assistance for our President's personal benefit, causing our allies to constantly "question the extent to which they can count on us."[181] Because American leadership depends on "the power of our example and the consistency of our purpose," President Trump's "conduct undermines the U.S., exposes our friends, and widens the playing field for autocrats like President Putin."[182] And President Trump's use of official acts to pressure Ukraine to announce politically motivated investigations harms our credibility in promoting democratic values and the rule of law in Ukraine and around the world. American credibility abroad "is based on a respect for the United States," and "if we damage that respect," American foreign policy cannot do its job.[183]

*   *   *

President Trump abused the powers of his office to invite foreign interference in an election for his own personal political gain and to the detriment of American national security interests. He abandoned his oath to faithfully execute the laws and betrayed his public trust. President Trump's misconduct presents a danger to our democratic processes, our national security, and our commitment to the rule of law. He must be removed from office.

II.   THE SENATE SHOULD CONVICT PRESIDENT TRUMP OF OBSTRUCTION OF CONGRESS

In exercising its responsibility to investigate and consider the impeachment of a President of the United States, the House is constitutionally entitled to the relevant information from the

---

[181] Transcript, *Impeachment Inquiry: Fiona Hill and David Holmes: Hearing Before the H. Permanent Select Comm. on Intelligence*, 116th Cong. 175 (Nov. 21, 2019).

[182] Transcript, *Impeachment Inquiry: Ambassador Marie "Masha" Yovanovitch: Hearing Before the H. Permanent Select Comm. on Intelligence*, 116th Cong. 19 (Nov. 15, 2019) (Yovanovitch Hearing Tr.).

[183] Transcript, *Impeachment Inquiry: Ambassador William B. Taylor and George Kent: Hearing Before the H. Permanent Select Comm. on Intelligence*, 116th Cong. 165 (Nov. 13, 2019).

Executive Branch concerning the President's misconduct.[184] The Framers, the courts, and past Presidents have recognized that honoring Congress's right to information in an impeachment investigation is a critical safeguard in our system of divided powers.[185] Otherwise, a President could hide his own wrongdoing to prevent Congress from discovering impeachable misconduct, effectively nullifying Congress's impeachment power.[186] President Trump's sweeping effort to shield his misconduct from view and protect himself from impeachment thus works a grave constitutional harm and is itself an impeachable offense.

A. The House Is Constitutionally Entitled to the Relevant Information in an Impeachment Inquiry

The House has the power to issue subpoenas and demand compliance in an impeachment investigation. The Supreme Court has long recognized that, "[w]ithout the power to investigate—including of course the authority to compel testimony, either through its own processes or through judicial trial—Congress could be seriously handicapped in its efforts to exercise its constitutional function wisely and effectively."[187] The Court has stressed that it is the "duty of all citizens" and "their unremitting obligation to respond to subpoenas, to respect the dignity of the Congress and its committees and to testify fully with respect to matters within the province of proper investigation."[188] The Court has repeatedly emphasized that Congress's "power of inquiry—with

---

[184] 4 Annals of Cong. 601 (1796) (statement of Rep. William Lyman) (noting that Congress has "the right to inspect every paper and transaction in any department" during an impeachment inquiry).

[185] *See, e.g., The Federalist No. 65* (Alexander Hamilton) (referring to the House as the "inquisitors for the nation" for purposes of impeachment); *Kilbourn v. Thompson*, 103 U.S. 168, 193 (1880); 4 James D. Richardson ed., Messages and Papers of Presidents 434-35 (1896); *see also* H. Rep. No. 116-346, at 139-42 (collecting examples of past Presidents beginning with George Washington acknowledging the importance of Congress's right to information from the Executive Branch in impeachment inquiries).

[186] *See generally* H. Rep. No. 116-346, at 139-48.

[187] *Quinn v. United States*, 349 U.S. 155, 160-61 (1955).

[188] *Watkins v. United States*, 354 U.S. 178, 187-88 (1957).

process to enforce it—is an essential and appropriate auxiliary to the legislative function."[189]

Congress "cannot legislate wisely or effectively in the absence of information."[190]

This principle is most compelling when the House exercises its "sole Power of Impeachment." Congress's already "broad" investigatory authority,[191] and its need for information, are at their apex in an impeachment inquiry. The principle that the President cannot stand in the way of an impeachment investigation is "of great consequence" because, as Supreme Court Justice Joseph Story long ago explained, "the president should not have the power of preventing a thorough investigation of [his] conduct, or of securing [himself] against the disgrace of a public conviction by impeachment, if [he] should deserve it."[192] A Presidential impeachment is "a matter of the most critical moment to the Nation" and it is "difficult to conceive of a more compelling need than that of this country for an unswervingly fair inquiry based on all the pertinent information."[193] The Supreme Court thus recognized nearly 140 years ago that where the House or Senate is determining a "question of . . . impeachment," there is "no reason to doubt the right to compel the attendance of witnesses, and their answer to proper questions, in the same manner and by the use of the same means that courts of justice can in like cases."[194]

Like the Supreme Court, members of the earliest Congresses understood that, without "the right to inspect every paper and transaction in any department . . . the power of impeachment could never be exercised with any effect."[195] Previous Presidents have acknowledged their obligation to

---

[189] *McGrain v. Daugherty*, 273 U.S. 135, 174 (1927).

[190] *Id.* at 175.

[191] *Watkins*, 354 U.S. at 187.

[192] 2 Joseph Story, *Commentaries on the Constitution of the United States* § 1501 (2d ed. 1851).

[193] *In re Report & Recommendation of June 5, 1972 Grand Jury Concerning Transmission of Evidence to House of Representatives*, 370 F. Supp. 1219, 1230 (D.D.C. 1974).

[194] *Kilbourn*, 103 U.S. at 190. The Court in *Kilbourn* invalidated a contempt order by the House but explained that the "whole aspect of the case would have changed" if it had been an impeachment proceeding. *Id.* at 193.

[195] 4 Annals of Cong. 601 (statement of Rep. William Lyman).

comply with an impeachment investigation, explaining that such an inquiry "penetrate[s] into the most secret recesses of the Executive Departments" and "could command the attendance of any and every agent of the Government, and compel them to produce all papers, public or private, official or unofficial, and to testify on oath to all facts within their knowledge."[196] That acknowledgement is a matter of common sense. An impeachment inquiry cannot root out bad actors if those same bad actors control the scope and nature of the inquiry.

President Trump is an aberration among Presidents in refusing any and all cooperation in a House impeachment investigation. Even President Nixon produced numerous documents in response to Congressional subpoenas and instructed "[a]ll members of the White House Staff . . . [to] appear voluntarily when requested by the [House]," to "testify under oath," and to "answer fully all proper questions"[197]—consistent with the near uniform cooperation of prior Executive Branch officials who had been subject to impeachment investigations.[198]

Because President Nixon's production of records in response to the House Judiciary Committee's inquiry was incomplete in important respects, however, the Committee voted to adopt an article of impeachment for his obstruction of the inquiry.[199] As the Committee explained, in refusing to provide materials that the Committee "deemed necessary" to the impeachment investigation, President Nixon had "substitute[ed] his judgment" for that of the House and interposed "the powers of the presidency against the lawful subpoenas of the House of Representatives, thereby assuming to himself functions and judgments necessary to exercise the sole

---

[196] Cong. Globe, 29th Cong., 1st Sess. 698 (1846) (statement of President James K. Polk); *see also* H. Rep. No. 116-346, at 139-42.

[197] Remarks by President Nixon (Apr. 17, 1973), *reprinted in Statement of Information: Hearings Before the Comm. on the Judiciary, H. of Representatives: Book IV—Part 2, Events Following the Watergate Break-in* (1974).

[198] H. Rep. No. 116-346, at 142; *see Impeachment of Richard M. Nixon, President of the United States: Report of the Comm. on the Judiciary, H. of Representatives*, H. Rep. No. 93-1305, at 196 (1974).

[199] *See* H. Rep. No. 93-1305, at 10.

33

power of impeachment vested by the Constitution in the House."[200] The Committee stated that it was not "within the power of the President to conduct an inquiry into his own impeachment, to determine which evidence, and what version or portion of that evidence, is relevant and necessary to such an inquiry. These are matters which, under the Constitution, the House has the sole power to determine."[201] In the face of Congress's investigation and the mounting evidence of his misdeeds, President Nixon resigned before the House had the chance to impeach him for this misconduct.

B. President Trump's Obstruction of the Impeachment Inquiry Violates Fundamental Constitutional Principles

The Senate should convict President Trump of Obstruction of Congress as charged in the Second Article of Impeachment. President Trump unilaterally declared the House's investigation "illegitimate."[202] President Trump's White House Counsel notified the House that "President Trump cannot permit his Administration to participate in this partisan inquiry under these circumstances."[203] President Trump then directed his Administration categorically to withhold documents and testimony from the House.

The facts are undisputed. As charged in the Second Article of Impeachment, President Trump "[d]irect[ed] the White House to defy a lawful subpoena by withholding the production of documents" to the Committees; "[d]irect[ed] other Executive Branch agencies and offices to defy lawful subpoenas and withhold the production of documents and records from the Committees"; and "[d]irected current and former Executive Branch officials not to cooperate with the Committees."[204] In response to President Trump's directives, OMB, the Department of State, Department of Energy, and Department of Defense refused to produce any documents to the

---

[200] *Id.* at 4.
[201] *Id.* at 194.
[202] *See* Statement of Facts ¶ 177.
[203] *See id.* ¶ 169.
[204] H. Res. 755, at 7; *see* Statement of Facts ¶ 169.

34

House, even though witness testimony has revealed that additional highly relevant records exist.[205] To date, the House Committees have not received a single document or record from these departments and agencies pursuant to subpoenas, which remain in effect.

President Trump personally demanded that his top aides refuse to testify in response to subpoenas, and nine Administration officials followed his directive and continue to defy subpoenas for testimony.[206] For example, when the Intelligence Committee issued a subpoena for Mick Mulvaney's testimony, he produced a November 8 letter from the White House stating: "the President directs Mr. Mulvaney not to appear at the Committee's scheduled deposition on November 8, 2019."[207] When President Trump was unable to silence witnesses, he resorted to tactics to penalize and intimidate them. These efforts include President Trump's sustained attacks on the anonymous whistleblower, and his public statements designed to discourage witnesses from coming forward and to embarrass those who did testify.[208]

Refusing to comply with a Congressional impeachment investigation is not a constitutionally valid decision for a President to make. President Trump's unprecedented "complete defiance of an impeachment inquiry . . . served to cover up the President's own repeated misconduct and to seize and control the power of impeachment."[209] President Trump's directive rejects one of the key features distinguishing our Republic from a monarchy: that "[t]he President of the United States [is] liable to be impeached, tried, and, upon conviction . . . removed."[210] Allowing President Trump to avoid conviction on the Second Article would set a dangerous precedent for future Presidents to

---

[205] Statement of Facts ¶¶ 179-83.
[206] *Id.* ¶¶ 186-87.
[207] *Id.* ¶ 186.
[208] *Id.* ¶ 190 & nn.309-10.
[209] H. Res. 755, at 8.
[210] *The Federalist No. 69* (Alexander Hamilton).

hide their misconduct from Congressional scrutiny during an impeachment inquiry without fear of accountability.

Notwithstanding President Trump's obstruction, the House obtained compelling evidence that he abused his power. The failure of President Trump's obstruction and attempted cover-up, however, does not excuse his misconduct. There can be no doubt that the withheld documents and testimony would provide Congress with highly pertinent information about the President's corrupt scheme. Indeed, witnesses have testified about specific withheld records concerning President Trump's July 25 call with President Zelensky and related materials,[211] and public reports have referred to additional responsive documents, including "hundreds of documents that reveal extensive efforts to generate an after-the-fact justification for" withholding the security aid.[212]

C. President Trump's Excuses for His Obstruction Are Meritless

President Trump has offered various unpersuasive excuses for his blanket refusal to comply with the House's impeachment inquiry. President Trump's refusal to provide information is not a principled assertion of executive privilege, but rather is a transparent attempt to cover-up wrongdoing and amass power that the Constitution does not give him, including the power to decide whether and when Congress can hold him accountable.

First, while Congressional investigators often accommodate legitimate Executive Branch interests, the President's blanket directive to all Executive Branch agencies and witnesses to defy Congressional subpoenas was not based on any actual assertion of executive privilege or

---

[211] *See* Statement of Facts ¶ 184 & nn.296-97.

[212] *Id.* ¶ 45. As noted above, the testimony of Messrs. Mulvaney, Blair, and Duffey would shed additional light on the White House's efforts to create an after-the-fact justification for the President's withholding of security assistance. Ambassador Bolton's testimony would likewise be illuminating in this regard given public reporting of his repeated, yet unsuccessful, efforts to convince the President to lift the hold.

identification of particular sensitive information.[213] The White House Counsel's letter alluded to "long-established Executive Branch confidentiality interests and privileges" that the State Department could theoretically invoke,[214] and the Justice Department's Office of Legal Counsel preemptively dismissed certain subpoenas as "invalid" on the ground that responsive information was "*potentially* protected by executive privilege."[215] But neither document conveyed an actual assertion of executive privilege,[216] which would require, at a minimum, identification by the President of particular communications or documents containing protected material.[217] The White House cannot justify a blanket refusal to respond to Congressional subpoenas based on an executive or other privilege it never in fact invoked.

Regardless, executive privilege is inapplicable here, both because it may not be used to conceal wrongdoing—particularly in an impeachment inquiry—and because the President and his agents have already diminished any confidentiality interests by speaking at length about these events in every forum except Congress.[218] President Trump has been impeached for Obstruction of Congress not based upon discrete invocations of privilege or immunity, but for his directive that the Executive Branch categorically stonewall the House impeachment inquiry by refusing to comply with all subpoenas.[219]

To the extent President Trump claims that he has concealed evidence to protect the Office of the President, the Framers considered and rejected that defense. Several delegates at the Constitutional Convention warned that the impeachment power would be "destructive of [the

---

[213] *See id.* ¶ 172.

[214] *Id.*

[215] *Id.*

[216] *Id.*

[217] *See, e.g., Landry v. Fed. Deposit Ins. Corp.*, 204 F.3d 1125, 1135 (D.C. Cir. 2000).

[218] *See, e.g., In re Sealed Case*, 121 F.3d 729, 738 (D.C. Cir. 1997); Statement of Facts ¶ 173 & n.280.

[219] *See* H. Res. 755, at 7.

executive's] independence."[220] But the Framers adopted an impeachment power anyway because, as Alexander Hamilton observed, "the powers relating to impeachments" are "an essential check in the hands of [Congress] upon the encroachments of the executive."[221] The impeachment power does not exist to protect the Presidency; it exists to protect the nation from a corrupt and dangerous President like Donald Trump.

Second, President Trump has no basis for objecting to how the House conducted its impeachment proceedings. The Constitution vests the House with the "sole Power of Impeachment"[222] and the power to "determine the Rules of its Proceedings."[223]

The rights that President Trump has demanded have never been recognized and have not been afforded in any prior Presidential impeachment.[224] President Trump has been afforded protections equal to or greater than those afforded Presidents Nixon and Clinton during their impeachment proceedings in the House.[225] Any claim that President Trump was entitled to due process rights modeled on a criminal trial during the entirety of the House impeachment inquiry ignores both law and history. A House impeachment inquiry cannot be compared to a criminal trial because the Senate, not the House, possesses the "sole Power to try Impeachments."[226] The Constitution does not entitle President Trump to a separate, full trial first in the House.

Even indulging the analogy to a criminal trial, no person appearing before a prosecutor or grand jury deciding whether to bring charges would have the rights President Trump has claimed.

---

[220] 2 Farrand at 67.

[221] *The Federalist No. 66* (Alexander Hamilton).

[222] U.S. Const., Art. I, § 2, cl. 5.

[223] U.S. Const., Art. I, § 5, cl. 2.

[224] *See, e.g.*, Statement of Facts ¶ 163; *see also* U.S. Const., Art. I, § 2, cl. 5.

[225] Statement of Facts ¶ 163; 165 Cong. Rec. E1357 (2019) (Impeachment Inquiry Procedures in the Committee on the Judiciary Pursuant to H. Res. 660); *Investigatory Powers of the Comm. on the Judiciary with Respect to its Impeachment Inquiry*, H. Rep. No. 105-795 (1998); H. Rep. No. 93-1305, at 8.

[226] U.S. Const., Art. I, § 3, cl. 6.

As the House Judiciary Committee Chairman observed during Watergate, "it is not a right but a privilege or a courtesy" for the President to participate through counsel in House impeachment proceedings.[227] President Trump's demands are just another effort to obstruct the House in the exercise of its constitutional duty.

Third, President Trump's assertion that his impeachment for obstruction of Congress is invalid because the Committees did not first seek judicial enforcement of their subpoenas ignores again the Constitutional dictate that the House has sole authority to determine how to proceed with an impeachment. It also ignores President Trump's own arguments to the federal courts.

President Trump is telling one story to Congress while spinning a different tale in the courts. He is saying to Congress that the Committees should have sued the Executive Branch in court to enforce their subpoenas. But he has argued to that court that Congressional Committees *cannot sue* the Executive Branch to enforce their subpoenas.[228] President Trump cannot tell Congress that it must pursue him in court, while simultaneously telling the courts that they are powerless to enforce Congressional subpoenas.

President Trump's approach to the Judicial Branch thus mirrors his obstruction of the Legislative Branch—in his view, neither can engage in any review of his conduct. This position conveys the President's dangerously misguided belief that no other branch of government may

---

[227] *Impeachment Inquiry: Hearings Before the H. Comm. on the Judiciary, Book I*, 93d Cong. 497 (1974) (statement of Chairman Peter W. Rodino, Jr.).

[228] *See* Statement of Facts ¶ 192; Def.'s Mot. to Dismiss, or in the Alternative, for Summ. J. at 20, *Kupperman v. U.S. House of Representatives*, No. 19-3224 (D.D.C. Nov. 14, 2019), ECF No. 40; Defs.' and Def.-Intervenors' Mot. to Dismiss at 46-47, *Comm. on Ways & Means v. U.S. Dep't of the Treasury*, No. 19-1974 (D.D.C. Sept. 6, 2019), ECF No. 44; *see also* Brief for Def.-Appellant at 2, 32-33, *Comm. on the Judiciary v. McGahn*, No. 19-5331 (D.C. Cir. Dec. 9, 2019).

check his power or hold him accountable for abusing it.[229] That belief is fundamentally incompatible with our form of government.

Months or years of litigation over each of the House's subpoenas is in any event no answer in this time-sensitive inquiry. The House's subpoena to former White House Counsel Don McGahn was issued in April 2019, but it is still winding its way through the courts over President Trump's strong opposition, even on an expedited schedule.[230] Litigating President Trump's direction that each subpoena be denied would conflict with the House's urgent duty to act on the compelling evidence of impeachable misconduct that it has uncovered. Further delay could also compromise the integrity of the 2020 election.

*　　*　　*

When the Framers entrusted the House with the sole power of impeachment, they obviously meant to equip the House with the necessary tools to discover abuses of power by the President. Without that authority, the Impeachment Clause would fail as an effective safeguard against tyranny. A system in which the President cannot be charged with a crime, as the Department of Justice believes, and in which he can nullify the impeachment power through blanket obstruction, as President Trump has done here, is a system in which the President is above the law. The Senate should convict President Trump for his categorical obstruction of the House's impeachment inquiry and ensure that this President, and any future President, cannot commit impeachable offenses and then avoid accountability by covering them up.

---

[229] *See also* Statement of Facts ¶ 164 ("I have an Article II, where I have the right to do whatever I want as president.").
[230] *See id.* ¶ 192 & n.316.

III. THE SENATE SHOULD IMMEDIATELY REMOVE PRESIDENT TRUMP FROM OFFICE TO PREVENT FURTHER ABUSES

President Trump has demonstrated his continued willingness to corrupt free and fair elections, betray our national security, and subvert the constitutional separation of powers—all for personal gain. President Trump's ongoing pattern of misconduct demonstrates that he is an immediate threat to the Nation and the rule of law. It is imperative that the Senate convict and remove him from office now, and permanently bar him from holding federal office.

A. President Trump's Repeated Abuse of Power Presents an Ongoing Threat to Our Elections

President Trump's solicitation of Ukrainian interference in the 2020 election is not an isolated incident. It is part of his ongoing and deeply troubling course of misconduct that, as the First Article of Impeachment states, is "consistent with President Trump's previous invitations of foreign interference in United States elections."[231]

These previous efforts include inviting Russian interference in the 2016 Presidential election.[232] As Special Counsel Mueller concluded, the "Russian government interfered in the 2016 presidential election in sweeping and systematic fashion."[233] Throughout the 2016 election cycle, the Trump Campaign maintained significant contacts with agents of the Russian government who were offering damaging information concerning then-candidate Trump's political opponent, and Mr. Trump repeatedly praised—and even publicly requested—the release of politically charged Russian-hacked emails.[234] The Trump Campaign welcomed Russia's election interference because it "expected it would benefit electorally from information stolen and released through Russian efforts."[235]

---

[231] H. Res. 755, at 5.
[232] Statement of Facts ¶¶ 191-93.
[233] *Id.* ¶ 13.
[234] *Id.* ¶¶ 152-56.
[235] *Id.* ¶ 152.

President Trump's recent actions confirm that public censure is insufficient to deter him from continuing to facilitate foreign interference in U.S. elections. In June 2019, President Trump declared that he sees "nothing wrong with listening" to a foreign power that offers information detrimental to a political adversary. In the President's words: "I think I'd take it."[236] Asked whether such information should be reported to law enforcement, President Trump retorted: "Give me a break, life doesn't work that way."[237]

Only one day after Special Counsel Mueller testified to Congress that the Trump Campaign welcomed and sought to capitalize on Russia's efforts to damage the President's political rival in 2016, President Trump spoke to President Zelensky, pressuring Ukraine to announce investigations to damage President Trump's political opponent in the 2020 election and undermine Special Counsel Mueller's findings.[238] President Trump still embraces that call as both "routine" and "perfect."[239] President Trump's conduct would have horrified the Framers of our republic.

In its findings, the Intelligence Committee emphasized the "proximate threat of further presidential attempts to solicit foreign interference in our next election."[240] That threat has not abated. In a sign that President Trump's corrupt efforts to encourage interference in the 2020 election persist, he reiterated his desire for Ukraine to investigate his political opponents even after the scheme was discovered and the impeachment inquiry was announced. When asked in October 2019 what he hoped President Zelensky would do about "the Bidens," President Trump answered

---

[236] *Id.* ¶ 156.
[237] *Id.*
[238] *Id.* ¶¶ 76, 157.
[239] *Id.* ¶ 77 n.132.
[240] H. Rep. No. 116-335, at XI.

that it was "very simple" and he hoped Ukraine would "start a major investigation."[241] Unsolicited, he added that "China should [likewise] start an investigation into the Bidens."[242]

President Trump has also continued to engage Mr. Giuliani to pursue the sham investigations on his behalf.[243] One day after President Trump was impeached, Mr. Giuliani claimed that he gathered derogatory evidence against Vice President Biden during a fact-finding trip to Ukraine—a trip where he met with a current Ukrainian official who attended a KGB school in Moscow and has led calls in Ukraine to investigate Burisma and the Bidens.[244] During the trip, Mr. Giuliani tweeted: "The conversation about corruption in Ukraine was based on compelling evidence of criminal conduct by then VP Biden, in 2016, that has not been resolved and until it is will be a major obstacle to the US assisting Ukraine with its anti-corruption reforms."[245] Not only was Mr. Giuliani perpetuating the false allegations against the former Vice President, but he was reiterating the threat that President Trump had used to pressure President Zelensky to announce the investigations: that U.S. assistance to Ukraine would be withheld until Ukraine pursued the sham investigations. Mr. Giuliani has stated that he and the President continue to be "on the same page."[246] Ukraine, as well, understands that Mr. Giuliani represents President Trump's interests.[247]

President Trump's unrepentant embrace of foreign election interference illustrates the threat posed by his continued occupancy of the Office of the President. It also refutes the assertion that the consequences of his misconduct should be decided by the voters in the 2020 election. The aim of President Trump's Ukraine scheme was to corrupt the integrity of the 2020 election by enlisting a foreign power to give him an unfair advantage—in short, to cheat. That threat persists today.

---

[241] Statement of Facts ¶ 142.
[242] *Id.*
[243] *See id.* ¶¶ 144-49.
[244] *Id.*
[245] *Id.* ¶ 146.
[246] *Id.* ¶ 149.
[247] *Id.* ¶¶ 19, 69, 89.

43

B.   President Trump's Obstruction of Congress Threatens Our Constitutional Order

President Trump's obstruction of the House's impeachment inquiry intended to hold him accountable for his misconduct presents a serious danger to our constitutional checks and balances.

President Trump has made clear that he refuses to accept Congress's express—and exclusive—constitutional role in conducting impeachments.[248] He has thereby subverted the Constitution that he pledged to uphold when he was inaugurated on the steps of the Capitol. By his words and deeds, President Trump has obstructed the House's impeachment inquiry at every turn: He has dismissed impeachment as "illegal, invalid, and unconstitutional";[249] directed the Executive Branch not to comply with House subpoenas for documents and testimony;[250] and intimidated and threatened the anonymous intelligence community whistleblower as well as the patriotic public servants who honored their subpoenas and testified before the House.[251]

President Trump's obstruction is part of an ominous pattern of efforts "to undermine United States Government investigations into foreign interference in United States elections."[252] Rather than assist Special Counsel Mueller's investigation into Russian interference in the 2016 election and his own campaign's exploitation of that foreign assistance, President Trump repeatedly used the powers of his office to impede it. Among other actions, President Trump directed the White House Counsel to fire the Special Counsel and then create a false record of the firing, tampered with witnesses in the Special Counsel's investigation, and repeatedly and publicly attacked the legitimacy of the investigation.[253] President Trump has instructed the former White House

---

[248] *See, e.g., id.* ¶¶ 169-71; U.S. Const., Art. I, § 2, cl. 5; U.S. Const., Art. I, § 3, cl. 6.
[249] Statement of Facts ¶ 177.
[250] *Id.* ¶ 169.
[251] *Id.* ¶ 177.
[252] H. Res. 755, at 7-8.
[253] *See* Statement of Facts ¶ 193.

Counsel to defy a House Committee's subpoena for testimony concerning these matters and the Department of Justice has argued that the courts cannot even hear the Committee's action to enforce its subpoena.[254]

President Trump's current obstruction of Congress is, therefore, not the first time he has committed misconduct concerning a federal investigation into election interference and then sought to hide it. Allowing this pattern to continue without repercussion would send the clear message that President Trump is correct in his view that *no* governmental body can hold him accountable for wrongdoing. That view is erroneous and exceptionally dangerous.

C. The Senate Should Convict and Remove President Trump to Protect Our System of Government and National Security Interests

The Senate should convict and remove President Trump to avoid serious and long-term damage to our democratic values and the Nation's security.

If the Senate permits President Trump to remain in office, he and future leaders would be emboldened to welcome, and even enlist, foreign interference in elections for years to come. When the American people's faith in their electoral process is shaken and its results called into question, the essence of democratic self-government is called into doubt.

Failure to remove President Trump would signal that a President's personal interests may take precedence over those of the Nation, alarming our allies and emboldening our adversaries. Our leadership depends on the power of our example and the consistency of our purpose," but because of President Trump's actions, "[b]oth have now been opened to question."[255]

Ratifying President Trump's behavior would likewise erode longstanding U.S. anti-corruption policy, which encourages countries to refrain from using the criminal justice system to

---

[254] *Id.* ¶ 192 & n.316.
[255] Yovanovitch Hearing Tr. at 19.

45

investigate political opponents. As many witnesses explained, urging Ukraine to engage in "selective politically associated investigations or prosecutions" undermines the power of America's example and our longstanding efforts to promote the rule of law abroad.[256]

An acquittal would also provide license to President Trump and his successors to use taxpayer dollars for personal political ends. Foreign aid is not the only vulnerable source of funding; Presidents could also hold hostage federal funds earmarked for States—such as money for natural disasters, highways, and healthcare—unless and until State officials perform personal political favors. Any Congressional appropriation would be an opportunity for a President to solicit a favor for his personal political purposes—or for others to seek to curry favor with him. Such an outcome would be entirely incompatible with our constitutional system of self-government.

* * *

President Trump has betrayed the American people and the ideals on which the Nation was founded. Unless he is removed from office, he will continue to endanger our national security, jeopardize the integrity of our elections, and undermine our core constitutional principles.

Respectfully submitted,

Adam B. Schiff
Jerrold Nadler
Zoe Lofgren
Hakeem S. Jeffries
Val Butler Demings
Jason Crow
Sylvia R. Garcia

January 18, 2020   *U.S. House of Representatives Managers**

---

[256] Statement of Facts ¶ 122.

* The House Managers wish to acknowledge the assistance of the following individuals in preparing this trial memorandum: Douglas N. Letter, Megan Barbero, Josephine Morse, Adam A. Grogg, William E. Havemann, and Jonathan B. Schwartz of the House Office of General Counsel; Daniel Noble, Daniel S. Goldman, and Maher Bitar of the House Permanent Select Committee on Intelligence; Norman L. Eisen, Barry H. Berke, Joshua Matz, and Sophia Brill of the House Committee on the Judiciary; the investigative staff of the House Committee on Oversight and Reform; and David A. O'Neil, Anna A. Moody, and Laura E. O'Neill.

46

IN THE SENATE OF THE UNITED STATES
Sitting as a Court of Impeachment

In re

**IMPEACHMENT OF
PRESIDENT DONALD J. TRUMP**

STATEMENT OF MATERIAL FACTS

**ATTACHMENT TO THE TRIAL MEMORANDUM
OF THE UNITED STATES HOUSE OF REPRESENTATIVES
IN THE IMPEACHMENT TRIAL OF PRESIDENT DONALD J. TRUMP**

TABLE OF CONTENTS

INTRODUCTION 1

STATEMENT OF MATERIAL FACTS 2

I.   President Trump's Abuse of Power 2

    A. The President's Scheme to Solicit Foreign Interference in the 2020 Election from the New Ukrainian Government Began in Spring 2019 2

    B. The President Enlisted His Personal Attorney and U.S. Officials to Help Execute the Scheme for His Personal Benefit 8

    C. The President Froze Vital Military and Other Security Assistance for Ukraine 11

    D. President Trump Conditioned a White House Meeting on Ukraine Announcing It Would Launch Politically Motivated Investigations 19

    E. President Trump Directly Solicited Election Interference from President Zelensky 25

    F. President Trump Conditioned the Release of Security Assistance for Ukraine, and Continued to Leverage a White House Meeting, to Pressure Ukraine to Launch Politically Motivated Investigations 29

    G. President Trump Was Forced to Lift the Hold but Has Continued to Solicit Foreign Interference in the Upcoming Election 39

    H. President Trump's Conduct Was Consistent with His Previous Invitations of Foreign Interference in U.S. Elections 47

II. President Trump's Obstruction of Congress 49

    A. The House Launched an Impeachment Inquiry 50

    B. President Trump Ordered Categorical Obstruction of the House's Impeachment Inquiry 51

    C. Following President Trump's Directive, the Executive Branch Refused to Produce Requested and Subpoenaed Documents 55

    D. President Trump Ordered Top Aides Not to Testify, Even Pursuant to Subpoena 58

    E. President Trump's Conduct Was Consistent with His Previous Efforts to Obstruct Investigations into Foreign Interference in U.S. Elections 60

INTRODUCTION

The U.S. House of Representatives has adopted Articles of Impeachment charging President Donald J. Trump with abuse of office and obstruction of Congress. The House's Trial Memorandum explains why the Senate should convict and remove President Trump from office, and permanently bar him from government service. The Memorandum relies on this Statement of Material Facts, which summarizes key evidence relating to the President's misconduct.

As further described below, and as detailed in House Committee reports,[1] President Trump used the powers of his office and U.S. taxpayers' money to pressure a foreign country, Ukraine, to interfere in the 2020 U.S. Presidential election on his behalf. President Trump's goals—which became known to multiple U.S. officials who testified before the House—were simple and starkly political: he wanted Ukraine's new President to announce investigations that would assist his 2020 reelection campaign and tarnish a political opponent, former Vice President Joseph Biden, Jr. As leverage, President Trump illegally withheld from Ukraine nearly $400 million in vital military and other security assistance that had been appropriated by Congress, and an official White House meeting that President Trump had promised Volodymyr Zelensky, the newly elected President of Ukraine. President Trump did this despite U.S. national security officials' unanimous opposition to withholding the aid from Ukraine, placing his own personal and political interests above the national security interests of the United States and undermining the integrity of our democracy.

When this scheme became known and Committees of the House launched an investigation, the President, for the first time in American history, ordered the categorical obstruction of an

---

[1] *See Report of the H. Permanent Select Comm. on Intelligence on the Trump-Ukraine Impeachment Inquiry, together with Minority Views*, H. Rep. No. 116-335 (2019); *Impeachment of Donald J. Trump, President of the United States: Report of the Comm. on the Judiciary of the H. of Representatives, together with Dissenting Views, to Accompany H. Res. 755*, H. Rep. No. 116-346 (2019).

impeachment inquiry. President Trump directed that no witnesses should testify and no documents should be produced to the House, a co-equal branch of government endowed by the Constitution with the "sole Power of Impeachment."[2] President Trump's conduct—both in soliciting a foreign country's interference in a U.S. election and then obstructing the ensuing investigation into that interference—was consistent with his prior conduct during and after the 2016 election.

STATEMENT OF MATERIAL FACTS

I.   PRESIDENT TRUMP'S ABUSE OF POWER

A.   The President's Scheme to Solicit Foreign Interference in the 2020 Election from the New Ukrainian Government Began in Spring 2019

1.   On April 21, 2019, Volodymyr Zelensky, a political neophyte, won a landslide victory in Ukraine's Presidential election.[3] Zelensky campaigned on an anti-corruption platform, and his victory reaffirmed the Ukrainian people's strong desire for reform.[4]

2.   When President Trump called to congratulate Zelensky later that day, President Trump did not raise any concerns about corruption in Ukraine, although his staff had prepared written materials for him recommending that he do so, and the White House call readout incorrectly indicated he did.[5]

---

[2] U.S. Const., Art. I, § 2, cl. 5.

[3] Transcript, Deposition of Lt. Colonel Alexander S. Vindman Before the H. Permanent Select Comm. on Intelligence 16 (Oct. 29, 2019) (Vindman Dep. Tr.); Anton Troianovski, *Comedian Volodymyr Zelensky Unseats Incumbent in Ukraine's Presidential Election, Exit Polls Show*, Wash. Post (Apr. 21, 2019), https://perma.cc/J8KE-2UJU.

[4] *Id.*

[5] *See* White House, *Memorandum of Telephone Conversation* (Apr. 21, 2019) (Apr. 21 Memorandum), https://perma.cc/EY4N-B8VS; Deb Riechmann et al., *Conflicting White House Accounts of 1st Trump-Zelenskiy Call*, Associated Press (Nov. 15, 2019), https://perma.cc/A6U9-89ZG.

3.   During the call, President Trump promised President-elect Zelensky that a high-level U.S. delegation would attend his inauguration and told him, "When you're settled in and ready, I'd like to invite you to the White House."[6]

4.   Both events would have demonstrated strong support by the United States as Ukraine fought a war—and negotiated for peace—with Russia. "Russia was watching closely to gauge the level of American support for the Ukrainian Government."[7] A White House visit also would have bolstered Zelensky's standing at home as he pursued his anti-corruption agenda.[8]

5.   Following the April 21 call, President Trump asked Vice President Mike Pence to lead the American delegation to President Zelensky's inauguration. During his own call with President-elect Zelensky on April 23, Vice President Pence confirmed that he would attend the inauguration "if the dates worked out."[9]

6.   On April 23, the media reported that former Vice President Biden was going to enter the 2020 race for the Democratic nomination for President of the United States.[10]

---

[6] Apr. 21 Memorandum at 2, https://perma.cc/EY4N-B8VS.

[7] Transcript, *Impeachment Inquiry: Ambassador William B. Taylor and George Kent: Hearing Before the H. Permanent Select Comm. on Intelligence*, 116th Cong. 40 (Nov. 13, 2019) (Taylor-Kent Hearing Tr.).

[8] *See, e.g.*, Transcript, Interview of Kurt Volker Before the H. Permanent Select Comm. on Intelligence 58-59 (Oct. 3, 2019) (Volker Interview Tr.); Transcript, Interview of George Kent Before the H. Permanent Select Comm. on Intelligence 202 (Oct. 15, 2019) (Kent Dep. Tr.); Transcript, Deposition of Fiona Hill Before the H. Permanent Select Comm. on Intelligence 64-65 (Oct. 14, 2019) (Hill Dep. Tr.); *see also* Transcript, Deposition of David A. Holmes Before the H. Permanent Select Comm. on Intelligence 18 (Nov. 15, 2019) (Holmes Dep. Tr.) ("[A] White House visit was critical to President Zelensky," because "[h]e needed to demonstrate U.S. support at the highest levels, both to advance his ambitious anti-corruption agenda at home and to encourage Russian President Putin to take seriously President Zelensky's peace efforts.").

[9] Transcript, Deposition of Jennifer Williams Before the H. Permanent Select Comm. on Intelligence 36-37 (Nov. 7, 2019) (Williams Dep. Tr.).

[10] Matt Viser, *Joe Biden to Enter 2020 Presidential Race with Thursday Video Announcement*, Wash. Post (Apr. 23, 2019), https://perma.cc/M2B9-6J48.

7.   The next day, April 24, the State Department executed President Trump's order to recall the U.S. ambassador to Ukraine, Marie "Masha" Yovanovitch, who was a well-regarded career diplomat and champion for anti-corruption reforms in Ukraine.[11]

8.   The removal of Ambassador Yovanovitch was the culmination of a months-long smear campaign waged by the President's personal lawyer, Rudy Giuliani, and other allies of the President.[12] The President also helped amplify the smear campaign.[13]

9.   Upon her return to the United States, Ambassador Yovanovitch was informed by State Department officials that there was no substantive reason or cause for her removal, but that President Trump had simply "lost confidence" in her.[14]

10.   Mr. Giuliani later disclosed the true motive for Ambassador Yovanovitch's removal: Mr. Giuliani "believed that [he] needed Yovanovitch out of the way" because "[s]he was going to make the investigations difficult for everybody."[15]

11.   Mr. Giuliani was referring to the two politically motivated investigations that President Trump solicited from Ukraine in order to assist his 2020 reelection campaign: one into former Vice President Biden and a Ukrainian gas company, Burisma Holdings, on whose board

---

[11] Transcript, *Impeachment Inquiry: Ambassador Marie "Masha" Yovanovitch: Hearing Before the H. Permanent Select Comm. on Intelligence*, 116th Cong. 21-22 (Nov. 15, 2019) (Yovanovitch Hearing Tr.); Transcript, *Impeachment Inquiry: Fiona Hill and David Holmes: Hearing Before the H. Permanent Select Comm. on Intelligence*, 116th Cong. 18-19 (Nov. 21, 2019) (Hill-Holmes Hearing Tr.); Holmes Dep. Tr. at 13-14, 142.

[12] *See, e.g.*, Taylor-Kent Hearing Tr. at 25; Yovanovitch Hearing Tr. at 21-22; Hill-Holmes Hearing Tr. at 19-21.

[13] *See, e.g.*, Donald J. Trump (@realDonaldTrump), Twitter (Mar. 20, 2019, 7:40 PM), https://perma.cc/D4UT-5M6F (referencing Sean Hannity's interview with John Solomon regarding his opinion piece in *The Hill* titled *As Russia Collusion Fades, Ukrainian Plot to Help Clinton Emerges* (Mar. 20, 2019), https://perma.cc/2M35-LUQE).

[14] Yovanovitch Hearing Tr. at 21-22, 34-35.

[15] Adam Entous, *The Ukrainian Prosecutor Behind Trump's Impeachment*, New Yorker (Dec. 16, 2019), https://perma.cc/5XMR-BS8L (quoting Mr. Giuliani).

Biden's son sat;[16] the other into a discredited conspiracy theory that Ukraine, not Russia, had

interfered in the 2016 U.S. election to help Hillary Clinton's campaign. One element of the latter

conspiracy theory was that CrowdStrike—a NASDAQ-listed cybersecurity firm based in Sunnyvale,

California, that the President erroneously believed was owned by a Ukrainian oligarch—had

colluded with the Democratic National Committee (DNC) to frame Russia and help the election

campaign of Hillary Clinton.[17]

12.   There was no factual basis for either investigation. As to the first, witnesses

unanimously testified that there was no credible evidence to support the allegations that, in late

2015, Vice President Biden corruptly encouraged Ukraine to remove then-Prosecutor General

Viktor Shokin because he was investigating Burisma.[18] Rather, Vice President Biden was carrying

out official U.S. policy—with bipartisan support[19]—and promoting anti-corruption reforms in

Ukraine because Shokin was viewed by the United States, its European partners, and the

International Monetary Fund to be ineffectual at prosecuting corruption and was himself corrupt.[20]

---

[16] *See* White House, *Memorandum of Telephone Conversation* 4 (July 25, 2019) (July 25 Memorandum), https://perma.cc/8JRD-6K9V; Kyle Cheney, *"Of Course I Did": Giuliani Acknowledges Asking Ukraine to Investigate Biden*, Politico (Sept. 19, 2019), https://perma.cc/J7PY-N3SG.

[17] July 25 Memorandum at 3, https://perma.cc/8JRD-6K9V; *see also Remarks by President Trump and President Putin of the Russian Federation in Joint Press Conference*, White House (July 16, 2018), https://perma.cc/6M5R-XW7F ("[A]ll I can do is ask the question. My people came to me, Dan Coates came to me and some others—they said they think it's Russia. I have President Putin; he just said it's not Russia. I will say this: I don't see any reason why it would be, but I really do want to see the server."); *Transcript of AP Interview with Trump*, Associated Press (Apr. 23, 2017), https://perma.cc/2EFT-84N8 ("TRUMP: . . . Why wouldn't (former Hillary Clinton campaign chairman John) Podesta and Hillary Clinton allow the FBI to see the server? They brought in another company that I hear is Ukrainian-based. AP: CrowdStrike? TRUMP: That's what I heard. I heard it's owned by a very rich Ukrainian, that's what I heard.").

[18] *See, e.g.*, Volker Interview Tr. at 203.

[19] *See, e.g.*, Press Release, Senator Rob Portman, Portman, Durbin, Shaheen, and Senate Ukraine Caucus Reaffirm Commitment to Help Ukraine Take on Corruption (Feb. 12, 2016), https://perma.cc/9WD2-CZ29 (quoting bipartisan letter urging then-President Poroshenko of Ukraine "to press ahead with urgent reforms to the Prosecutor General's office and judiciary").

[20] *See, e.g.*, Kent Dep. Tr. at 45, 91-94 (describing "a broad-based consensus" among the United States, European allies, and international financial institutions that Mr. Shokin was "a typical

In fact, witnesses unanimously testified that the removal of Shokin made it *more likely* that Ukraine would investigate corruption, including Burisma and its owner, not less likely.[21] The Ukrainian Parliament removed Shokin in March 2016.[22]

13.   As to the second investigation, the U.S. Intelligence Community determined that Russia—not Ukraine—interfered in the 2016 election.[23] The Senate Select Committee on Intelligence reached the same conclusion following its own lengthy bipartisan investigation.[24] Special Counsel Robert Mueller, III, likewise concluded that the "Russian government interfered in the 2016 presidential election in sweeping and systematic fashion."[25] And FBI Director Christopher

---

Ukraine prosecutor who lived a lifestyle far in excess of his government salary, who never prosecuted anybody known for having committed a crime" and who "covered up crimes that were known to have been committed."); Daryna Krasnolutska et al., *Ukraine Prosecutor Says No Evidence of Wrongdoing by Bidens*, Bloomberg (May 16, 2019), https://perma.cc/YYX8-U33C (quoting Yuriy Lutsenko, Ukraine's then-Prosecutor General: "Hunter Biden did not violate any Ukrainian laws—at least as of now, we do not see any wrongdoing. A company can pay however much it wants to its board . . . . Biden was definitely not involved . . . . We do not have any grounds to think that there was any wrongdoing starting from 2014 [when Hunter Biden joined the board of Burisma].").

[21] *See* Kent Dep. Tr. at 45, 93-94; Volker Interview Tr. at 36-37, 330, 355.

[22] *See* Kent Dep. Tr. at 101-02.

[23] Office of the Dir. of Nat'l Intelligence, ICA 2017-01D, *Assessing Russian Activities and Intentions in Recent U.S. Elections* (Jan. 6, 2017), https://perma.cc/M4A3-DWML; *see, e.g., id.* at ii ("We assess Russian President Vladimir Putin ordered an influence campaign in 2016 aimed at the US presidential election. Russia's goals were to undermine public faith in the US democratic process, denigrate Secretary Clinton, and harm her electability and potential presidency. We further assess Putin and the Russian Government developed a clear preference for President-elect Trump. We have high confidence in these judgements.").

[24] Senate Select Comm. on Intelligence, *Russian Active Measures Campaigns and Interference in the 2016 U.S. Election, Vol. II* (May 8, 2018), https://perma.cc/96EC-22RU; *see, e.g., id.* at 4-5 ("The Committee found that the [Russian-based Internet Research Agency (IRA)] sought to influence the 2016 U.S. presidential election by harming Hillary Clinton's chances of success and supporting Donald Trump at the direction of the Kremlin. . . . The Committee found that the Russian government tasked and supported the IRA's interference in the 2016 U.S. election.").

[25] Robert S. Mueller III, *Report on the Investigation into Russian Interference in the 2016 Presidential Election*, Vol. I at 1 (2019) (Mueller Report), https://perma.cc/DN3N-9UW8.

Wray, a Trump appointee, recently confirmed that law enforcement "ha[s] no information that indicates that Ukraine interfered with the 2016 presidential election."[26]

14. As Dr. Fiona Hill—who served until July 2019 as the Senior Director of European and Russian Affairs at the National Security Council (NSC) under President Trump until July 2019—testified, the theory of Ukrainian interference in the 2016 election is a "fictional narrative that is being perpetrated and propagated by the Russian security services themselves" to deflect from Russia's own culpability and to drive a wedge between the United States and Ukraine.[27] In fact, shortly after the 2016 U.S. election, this conspiracy theory was promoted by none other than President Vladimir Putin himself.[28] On May 3, 2019, shortly after President Zelensky's election, President Trump and President Putin spoke by telephone, including about the so-called "'Russian Hoax.'"[29]

15. President Trump's senior advisors had attempted to dissuade the President from promoting this conspiracy theory, to no avail. Dr. Hill testified that President Trump's former Homeland Security Advisor Tom Bossert and former National Security Advisor H.R. McMaster "spent a lot of time trying to refute this [theory] in the first year of the administration."[30] Bossert

---

[26] Luke Barr & Alexander Mallin, *FBI Director Pushes Back on Debunked Conspiracy Theory About 2016 Election Interference*, ABC News (Dec. 9, 2019), https://perma.cc/8JKC-6RB8 (quoting Mr. Wray).

[27] Hill-Holmes Hearing Tr. at 40-41, 56-57.

[28] Press Statement, President of Russ., Joint News Conference with Hungarian Prime Minister Viktor Orban (Feb. 2, 2017), https://perma.cc/5Z2R-ZECB ("[A]s we all know, during the presidential campaign in the United States, the Ukrainian government adopted a unilateral position in favour of one candidate. More than that, certain oligarchs, certainly with the approval of the political leadership, funded this candidate, or female candidate, to be more precise.").

[29] *See* Kent Dep. Tr. at 338; @realDonaldTrump (May 3, 2019, 10:06 AM) https://perma.cc/7LS9-P35U.

[30] Hill Dep. Tr. at 234; *see also id.* at 235.

later said the false narrative about Ukrainian interference in the 2016 election was "not only a conspiracy theory, it is completely debunked."[31]

B. The President Enlisted His Personal Attorney and U.S. Officials to Help Execute the Scheme for His Personal Benefit

16. Shortly after his April 21 call with President Zelensky, President Trump began to publicly press for the two investigations he wanted Ukraine to pursue. On April 25—the day that former Vice President Biden announced his candidacy for the Democratic nomination for President—President Trump called into Sean Hannity's prime time *Fox News* show. Referencing alleged Ukrainian interference in the 2016 election, President Trump said, "It sounds like big stuff," and suggested that the Attorney General might investigate.[32]

17. On May 6, in a separate *Fox News* interview, President Trump claimed Vice President Biden's advocacy for Mr. Shokin's dismissal in 2016 was "a very serious problem" and "a major scandal, major problem."[33]

18. On May 9, the *New York Times* reported that Mr. Giuliani was planning to travel to Ukraine to urge President Zelensky to pursue the investigations.[34] Mr. Giuliani acknowledged that "[s]omebody could say it's improper" to pressure Ukraine to open investigations that would benefit President Trump, but he argued:

> [T]his isn't foreign policy—I'm asking them to do an investigation that they're doing already, and that other people are telling them to stop. And I'm going to give them reasons why they shouldn't stop it because

---

[31] Chris Francescani, *President Trump's Former National Security Advisor "Deeply Disturbed" by Ukraine Scandal: "Whole World Is Watching,"* ABC News (Sept. 29, 2019), https://perma.cc/C76K-7SMA (quoting Mr. Bossert).

[32] *Full Video: Sean Hannity Interviews Trump on Biden, Russia Probe, FISA Abuse, Comey,* Real Clear Politics (Apr. 26, 2019), https://perma.cc/3CLR-9MVA.

[33] *Transcript: Fox News Interview with President Trump,* Fox News (May 6, 2019), https://perma.cc/NST6-X7WS.

[34] Kenneth P. Vogel, *Rudy Giuliani Plans Ukraine Trip to Push for Inquiries That Could Help Trump,* N.Y. Times (May 9, 2019) (*Giuliani Plans Ukraine Trip*), https://perma.cc/SC6J-4PL9.

that information will be very, very helpful to my client, and may turn out to be helpful to my government.[35]

Ukraine was not, in fact, "already" conducting these investigations. As described below, the Trump Administration repeatedly tried but failed to get Ukrainian officials to instigate these investigations. According to Mr. Giuliani, the President supported his actions, stating that President Trump "basically knows what I'm doing, sure, as his lawyer."[36]

19.   In a letter dated May 10, 2019, and addressed to President-elect Zelensky, Mr. Giuliani wrote that he "represent[ed] him [President Trump] as a private citizen, not as President of the United States." In his capacity as "personal counsel to President Trump, and with his knowledge and consent," Mr. Giuliani requested a meeting with President Zelensky the following week to discuss a "specific request."[37]

20.   On the evening of Friday, May 10, however, Mr. Giuliani announced that he was canceling his trip.[38] He later explained, "I'm not going to go" to Ukraine "because I'm walking into a group of people that are enemies of the President."[39]

21.   By the following Monday morning, May 13, President Trump had ordered Vice President Pence not to attend President Zelensky's inauguration in favor of a lower-ranking delegation led by Secretary of Energy Rick Perry.[40]

---

[35] *Id.* (quoting Mr. Giuliani).

[36] *Id.* (quoting Mr. Giuliani).

[37] Lev Parnas Production to the House Permanent Select Comm. on Intelligence at 28 (Jan. 14, 2019), https://perma.cc/PWX4-LEMS (letter from Rudolph Giuliani to Volodymyr Zelensky, President-elect of Ukraine (May 10, 2019)).

[38] *See* Andrew Restuccia & Darren Samuelsohn, *Giuliani Cancels Ukraine Trip amid Political Meddling Charges*, Politico (May 11, 2019), https://perma.cc/V5S8-2FV4.

[39] *Giuliani: I Didn't Go to Ukraine to Start an Investigation, There Already Was One*, Fox News (May 11, 2019), https://perma.cc/HT7V-2ZYA.

[40] Williams Dep. Tr. at 37; Volker Interview Tr. at 288-90; Vindman Dep. Tr. at 125-27.

22.   The U.S. delegation—which also included Ambassador to the European Union Gordon Sondland, Special Representative for Ukraine Negotiations Ambassador Kurt Volker, and NSC Director for Ukraine Lieutenant Colonel Alexander Vindman—returned from the inauguration convinced that President Zelensky was genuinely committed to anti-corruption reforms.[41]

23.   At a meeting in the Oval Office on May 23, members of the delegation relayed their positive impressions to President Trump and encouraged him to schedule the promised Oval Office meeting for President Zelensky. President Trump, however, said he "didn't believe" the delegation's positive assessment, claiming "that's not what I hear" from Mr. Giuliani.[42] The President cast his dim view of Ukraine in personal terms, stating that Ukraine "tried to take me down" during the 2016 election—an apparent reference to the debunked conspiracy theory that Ukraine interfered in the 2016 election to help Hillary Clinton and harm his campaign.[43]

24.   Rather than commit to a date for an Oval Office meeting with President Zelensky, President Trump directed the delegation to "[t]alk to Rudy, talk to Rudy."[44] Ambassador Sondland testified that "if [the delegation] never called Rudy and just left it alone nothing would happen with Ukraine," and "if [the President] was going to have his mind changed, that was the path."[45] Following the May 23 meeting, Secretary Perry and Ambassadors Sondland and Volker began to coordinate and work with Mr. Giuliani to satisfy the President's demands.[46]

---

[41] Volker Interview Tr. at 29–30, 304.

[42] *Id.* at 305.

[43] *Id.* at 304; Transcript, Interview of Gordon Sondland Before the H. Permanent Select Comm. on Intelligence 337 (Oct. 17, 2019) (Sondland Dep. Tr.).

[44] Sondland Dep. Tr. at 62, 69-70; Volker Interview Tr. at 305; Transcript, *Impeachment Inquiry: Ambassador Kurt Volker and Timothy Morrison: Hearing Before the H. Permanent Select Comm. on Intelligence*, 116th Cong. 39-40 (Nov. 19, 2019) (Volker-Morrison Hearing Tr.).

[45] Sondland Dep. Tr. at 90.

[46] *See id.* at 77-78; Volker-Morrison Hearing Tr. at 17, 19; *see also* Timothy Puko & Rebecca Ballhaus, *Rick Perry Called Rudy Giuliani at Trump's Direction on Ukraine Concerns*, Wall Street J. (Oct. 16, 2019) (*Rick Perry Called Rudy Giuliani*), https://perma.cc/E4F2-9U23.

25.   Mr. Giuliani is not a U.S. government official and has never served in the Trump Administration. Rather, as he has repeatedly made clear, his goal was to obtain "information [that] will be very, very helpful to my client"—President Trump.[47] Mr. Giuliani made clear to Ambassadors Sondland and Volker, who were in direct communications with Ukrainian officials, that a White House meeting would not occur until Ukraine announced its pursuit of the two political investigations.[48]

26.   On June 17, Ambassador Bill Taylor, whom Secretary of State Mike Pompeo had asked to replace Ambassador Yovanovitch, arrived in Kyiv as the new Chargé d'Affaires.[49]

27.   Ambassador Taylor quickly observed that there was an "irregular channel" led by Mr. Giuliani that, over time, began to undermine the official channel of U.S. diplomatic relations with Ukraine.[50] Ambassador Sondland similarly testified that the agenda described by Mr. Giuliani became more "insidious" over time.[51] Mr. Giuliani would prove to be, as the President's National Security Advisor Ambassador John Bolton told a colleague, a "hand grenade that was going to blow everyone up."[52]

C.   The President Froze Vital Military and Other Security Assistance for Ukraine

28.   Since 2014, Ukraine has been engaged in an ongoing armed conflict with Russia in the Donbas region of eastern Ukraine.[53] Ukraine is a "strategic partner of the United States," and

---

[47] *Giuliani Plans Ukraine Trip*, https://perma.cc/SC6J-4PL9.

[48] *See, e.g.*, Transcript, *Impeachment Inquiry: Ambassador Sondland: Hearing Before the H. Permanent Select Comm. on Intelligence*, 116th Cong. 18 (Nov. 20, 2019) (Sondland Hearing Tr.) ("[A]s I testified previously . . . Mr. Giuliani's requests were a quid pro quo for arranging a White House visit for President Zelensky"); *id.* at 34, 42-43.

[49] Transcript, Deposition of William B. Taylor Before the H. Permanent Select Comm. on Intelligence (Oct. 22, 2019) (Taylor Dep. Tr.).

[50] Taylor-Kent Hearing Tr. at 34-36.

[51] Sondland Dep. Tr. at 240.

[52] Hill Dep. Tr. at 127 (Dr. Hill, quoting Mr. Bolton).

[53] *See* Taylor Dep. Tr. at 20, 23, 27-28, 31, 33-34; Transcript, Deposition of Ambassador Marie "Masha" Yovanovitch Before the H. Permanent Select Comm. on Intelligence 16, 18, 73, 302

the United States has long supported Ukraine in its conflict with Russia.[54] As Ambassador Volker and multiple other witnesses testified, supporting Ukraine is "critically important" to U.S. interests, including countering Russian aggression in the region.[55]

29.   Ukrainians face casualties on a near-daily basis in their ongoing conflict with Russia.[56] Since 2014, Russian aggression has resulted in more than 13,000 Ukrainian deaths on Ukrainian territory,[57] including approximately 3,331 civilians, and has wounded another 30,000 persons.[58]

30.   Since 2014, following Russia's invasion of Ukraine and its annexation of the Crimean Peninsula, Congress has allocated military and other security assistance funds to Ukraine on a broad bipartisan basis.[59] Since 2014, the United States has provided approximately $3.1 billion in foreign assistance to Ukraine: $1.5 billion in military and other security assistance, and $1.6 billion in non-military, non-humanitarian aid to Ukraine.[60]

(Oct. 11, 2019) (Yovanovitch Dep. Tr.); *see also Conflict in Ukraine Enters Its Fourth Year with No End in Sight*, Office of the U.N. High Comm'r for Human Rights (June 13, 2017), https://perma.cc/K9N8-F22E.

[54] Taylor-Kent Hearing Tr. at 28.

[55] Volker Interview Tr. at 329; *see* Yovanovitch Hearing Tr. at 17-18; Volker-Morrison Hearing Tr. at 11.

[56] Transcript, Deposition of Catherine Croft Before the H. Permanent Select Comm. on Intelligence 16 (Oct. 30, 2019) (Croft Dep. Tr.).

[57] Kent Dep. Tr. at 338-39.

[58] Viacheslav Shramovych, *Ukraine's Deadliest Day: The Battle of Ilovaisk, August 2014*, BBC News (Aug. 29, 2019), https://perma.cc/6B2F-B72W.

[59] *See* Transcript, Deposition of Laura Katherine Cooper Before the H. Permanent Select Comm. on Intelligence 16, 38, 98 (Oct. 23, 2019) (Cooper Dep. Tr.); Vindman Dep. Tr. at 41, 57, 165; Transcript, Deposition of Mark Sandy Before the H. Permanent Select Comm. on Intelligence 59-60 (Nov. 16, 2019) (Sandy Dep. Tr.); Taylor-Kent Hearing Tr. at 29-30; Taylor Dep. Tr. at 38, 40-41, 171, 217-18, 281-82; Letter from Senators Jeanne Shaheen et al. to Acting White House Chief of Staff Mick Mulvaney (Sept. 3, 2019) (Sept. 3 Letter), https://perma.cc/4TU8-H7UR; Letter from Senator Christopher Murphy to Chairman Adam B. Schiff, House Permanent Select Comm. on Intelligence, and Acting Chairwoman Carolyn Maloney, House Comm. on Oversight and Reform (Nov. 19, 2019) (Nov. 19 Letter), https://perma.cc/4BDP-2SRJ.

[60] Cory Welt, Cong. Research Serv., R45008, *Ukraine: Background, Conflict with Russia, and U.S. Policy* 30 (Sept. 19, 2019), https://perma.cc/4HCR-VKA5; *see also* Hill-Holmes Hearing Tr. at 97

31.   The military assistance provided by the United States to Ukraine "saves lives" by making Ukrainian resistance to Russia more effective.[61] It likewise advances U.S. national security interests because, "[i]f Russia prevails and Ukraine falls to Russian dominion, we can expect to see other attempts by Russia to expand its territory and influence."[62] Indeed, the reason the United States provides assistance to the Ukrainian military is "so that they can fight Russia over there, and we don't have to fight Russia here."[63]

32.   The United States' European allies have similarly provided political and economic support to Ukraine. Since 2014, the European Union (EU) has been the largest donor to Ukraine.[64] The EU has extended more macro-financial assistance to Ukraine—approximately €3.3 billion— than to any other non-EU country and has committed to extend another €1.1 billion.[65] Between 2014 and September 30, 2019, the EU and the European financial institutions (including the European Investment Bank, European Bank for Reconstruction and Development, and others) committed over €15 billion in grants and loans to support the reform process in Ukraine.[66] According to EU data, Germany contributed €786.5 million to Ukraine between 2014 and 2017; the United Kingdom contributed €105.6 million; and France contributed €61.9 million over that same period (not including the amounts these countries contribute through the EU).[67]

(testimony of David Holmes) ("The United States has provided combined civilian and military assistance to Ukraine since 2014 of about $3 billion, plus two $1 billion—three $1 billion loan guarantees. That is not—those get paid back largely. So just over $3 billion.").

[61] Taylor Dep. Tr. at 153.

[62] Yovanovitch Hearing Tr. at 18.

[63] Volker-Morrison Hearing Tr. at 11.

[64] Iain King, *Not Contributing Enough? A Summary of European Military and Development Assistance to Ukraine Since 2014*, Ctr. for Strategic & Int'l Stud. (Sept. 26, 2019), https://perma.cc/FF6F-Q9MX.

[65] *EU-Ukraine Relations—Factsheet*, European External Action Serv. (Sept. 30, 2019), https://perma.cc/4YKE-T2WT.

[66] *Id.*

[67] *See EU Aid Explorer: Donors*, European Comm'n, https://perma.cc/79H6-AFHY.

33.   In 2017 and 2018, the United States provided approximately $511 million and $359 million, respectively, in foreign assistance to Ukraine, including military and other security assistance.[68] During those two years, President Trump and his Administration allowed the funds to flow to Ukraine unimpeded.[69]

34.   For fiscal year 2019, Congress appropriated and authorized $391 million in taxpayer-funded security assistance to Ukraine: $250 million in funds administered by the Department of Defense (DOD) and $115 million in funds administered by the State Department, with another $26 million carried over from fiscal year 2018.[70]

35.   DOD planned to use the funds to provide Ukraine with sniper rifles, rocket-propelled grenade launchers, counter-artillery radars, electronic warfare detection and secure communications, and night vision equipment, among other military equipment, to defend itself against Russian forces, which have occupied part of eastern Ukraine since 2014.[71] These purposes were consistent with the goals of Congress, which had appropriated the funds administered by DOD under the Ukraine Security Assistance Initiative (USAI) for the purpose of providing "training; equipment; lethal assistance; logistics support, supplies and services; sustainment; and

---

[68] *U.S. Foreign Aid by Country*, USAID, https://perma.cc/9YK2-9BKJ (last updated Sept. 23, 2019) (Ukraine data for fiscal year 2017 and fiscal year 2018).

[69] Transcript, *Impeachment Inquiry: Ms. Laura Cooper and Mr. David Hale: Hearing Before the H. Permanent Select Comm. on Intelligence*, 116th Cong. 22-23 (Nov. 20, 2019) (Cooper-Hale Hearing Tr.); Cooper Dep. Tr. at 95-96.

[70] Department of Defense and Labor, Health and Human Services, and Education Appropriations Act, 2019 and Continuing Appropriations Act, 2019, Pub. L. No. 115-245, § 9013 (2018); Consolidated Appropriations Act, 2019, Pub. L. No. 116-6, § 7046(a)(2) (2019); *Conference Report to Accompany H.J. Res. 31*, H. Rep. No. 116-9, at 869 (2019) (allocating $115,000,000 in assistance to Ukraine for the Foreign Military Financing Program); Aaron Mehta, *U.S. State Department Clears Ukraine Security Assistance Funding. Is the Pentagon Next?*, Def. News (Sept. 12, 2019), https://perma.cc/723T-9XUN (noting that approximately $26 million rolled over from fiscal year 2018).

[71] Press Release, Dep't of Def., DOD Announces $250M to Ukraine, (June 18, 2019) (DOD Announces $250M to Ukraine), https://perma.cc/U4HX-ZKXP.

intelligence support to the military and national security forces of Ukraine, and . . . replacement of any weapons or articles provided to the Government of Ukraine."[72]

36.   On June 18, 2019, after all Congressionally mandated conditions on the DOD-administered aid—including certification that Ukraine had adopted sufficient anti-corruption reforms—were met, DOD issued a press release announcing its intention to provide the $250 million in security assistance to Ukraine.[73]

37.   On June 19, the Office of Management and Budget (OMB) received questions from President Trump about the funding for Ukraine.[74] OMB, in turn, made inquiries with DOD.[75]

38.   On June 27, Acting Chief of Staff Mick Mulvaney reportedly emailed his senior advisor Robert Blair, "Did we ever find out about the money for Ukraine and whether we can hold it back?" Mr. Blair responded that it would be possible, but they should "[e]xpect Congress to become unhinged" if the President held back the appropriated funds.[76]

39.   Around this time, despite overwhelming support for the security assistance from every relevant Executive Branch agency,[77] and despite the fact that the funds had been authorized

---

[72] Pub. L. No. 115-245, § 9013.

[73] DOD Announces $250M to Ukraine, https://perma.cc/U4HX-ZKXP. DOD had certified in May 2019 that Ukraine satisfied all anti-corruption standards needed to receive the Congressionally appropriated military aid. *See* Letter from John C. Rood, Under Sec'y of Def. for Pol'y, Dep't of Def., to Chairman Eliot L. Engel, House Comm. on Foreign Affairs (May 23, 2019), https://perma.cc/68FS-ZXZ6 ("Ukraine has taken substantial actions to make defense institutional reforms for the purposes of decreasing corruption . . . . [N]ow that this defense institution reform has occurred, we will use the authority provided . . . to support programs in Ukraine further.").

[74] Sandy Dep. Tr. at 24-25; Cooper Dep. Tr. at 33-34.

[75] Sandy Dep. Tr. at 24-28.

[76] Eric Lipton et al., *Behind the Ukraine Aid Freeze: 84 Days of Conflict and Confusion*, N.Y. Times (Dec. 29, 2019) (*Behind the Ukraine Aid Freeze*), https://perma.cc/TA5J-NJFX.

[77] *See, e.g.*, Cooper Dep. Tr. at 13, 16, 32, 46, 60-62, 64-65; Taylor Dep. Tr. at 28, 132, 170.

and appropriated by Congress with strong bipartisan support,[78] the President ordered a hold on all military and other security assistance for Ukraine.[79]

40. By July 3, OMB had blocked the release of $141 million in State Department funds. By July 12, all military and other security assistance for Ukraine had been blocked.[80]

41. On July 18, OMB announced to the relevant Executive Branch agencies during a secure videoconference that President Trump had ordered a hold on all Ukraine security assistance.[81] No explanation for the hold was provided.[82]

42. On July 25—approximately 90 minutes after President Trump spoke by phone with President Zelensky—OMB's Associate Director for National Security Programs, Michael Duffey, a political appointee, instructed DOD officials: "Based on guidance I have received and in light of the Administration's plan to review assistance to Ukraine, including the Ukraine Security Assistance Initiative, please hold off on any additional DoD obligations of these funds, pending direction from that process."[83] He added: "Given the sensitive nature of the request, I appreciate your keeping that information closely held to those who need to know to execute the direction."[84]

---

[78] *See* Nov. 19 Letter, https://perma.cc/4BDP-2SRJ; Sept. 3 Letter, https://perma.cc/4TU8-H7UR.

[79] Williams Dep. Tr. at 54; Croft Dep. Tr. at 15; Kent Dep. Tr. at 303-305; Transcript, Deposition of Ambassador David Maclain Hale Before the H. Permanent Select Comm. on Intelligence 81 (Oct. 31, 2019) (Hale Dep. Tr.); Sandy Dep. Tr. at 99; Vindman Dep. Tr. at 181-82; Transcript, Deposition of Ambassador Tim Morrison Before the H. Permanent Select Comm. on Intelligence 264 (Nov. 6, 2019) (Morrison Dep. Tr.).

[80] Cooper-Hale Hearing Tr. at 14; Vindman Dep. Tr. at 178-79; *see also Stalled Ukraine Military Aid Concerned Members of Congress for Months*, CNN (Sept. 30, 2019), https://perma.cc/5CHF-HFKJ; Sandy Dep. Tr. at 38-39 (describing July 12 email from White House to OMB stating "that the President is directing a hold on military support funding for Ukraine.").

[81] *See* Sandy Dep. Tr. at 90; Hill Dep. Tr. at 225; Taylor-Kent Hearing Tr. at 35; Vindman Dep. Tr. at 181; Holmes Dep. Tr. at 153-54.

[82] Taylor-Kent Hearing Tr. at 35; Hill Dep. Tr. at 225.

[83] Email from Michael Duffey, Assoc. Dir. for Nat'l Sec. Programs, Office of Mgmt. & Budget, to David Norquist et al. (July 25, 2019, 11:04 AM), https://perma.cc/PG93-3M6B.

[84] *Id.*

43.   In late July, the NSC convened a series of interagency meetings during which senior Executive Branch officials discussed the hold on security assistance.[85] Over the course of these meetings, a number of facts became clear: (1) the President personally directed the hold through OMB;[86] (2) no credible justification was provided for the hold;[87] (3) with the exception of OMB, all relevant agencies supported the Ukraine security assistance because, among other things, it was in the national security interests of the United States;[88] and (4) there were serious concerns about the legality of the hold.[89]

44.   Although President Trump later claimed that the hold was part of an effort to get European allies to share more of the costs for security assistance for Ukraine, officials responsible for the security assistance testified they had not heard that rationale discussed in June, July, or August. For example, Mark Sandy, OMB's Deputy Associate Director for National Security Programs, who is responsible for DOD's portion of the Ukraine security assistance, testified that the European burden-sharing explanation was first provided to him in September—following his

---

[85] Kent Dep. Tr. at 303, 307, 311; Taylor-Kent Hearing Tr. at 36; Vindman Dep. Tr. at 182-85, Cooper Dep. Tr. at 45.

[86] Kent Dep. Tr. at 303-305; Hale Dep. Tr. at 81.

[87] Croft Dep. Tr. at 15; Hale Dep. Tr. at 105; Holmes Dep. Tr. at 21; Kent Dep. Tr. at 304, 310; Cooper Dep. Tr. at 44-45; Sandy Dep. Tr. at 91, 97; Morrison Dep. Tr. at 162-63. Mr. Morrison testified that, during a Deputies Committee meeting on July 26, OMB stated that the "President was concerned about corruption in Ukraine, and he wanted to make sure that Ukraine was doing enough to manage that corruption." Morrison Dep. Tr. at 165. Mr. Morrison did not testify that concerns about Europe's contributions were raised during this meeting. In addition, Mark Sandy testified that, as of July 26, despite OMB's own statement, senior OMB officials were unaware of the reason for the hold at that time. *See* Sandy Dep. Tr. at 55-56.

[88] Sandy Dep. Tr. at 99; Vindman Dep. Tr. at 181-82; Kent Dep. Tr. at 305; Morrison Dep. Tr. at 264.

[89] Morrison Dep. Tr. at 163; Cooper Dep. Tr. at 47-48. For example, Deputy Assistant Secretary of Defense Laura Cooper testified that, during an interagency meeting on July 26 involving senior leadership from the State Department and DOD and officials from the National Security Council, "immediately deputies began to raise concerns about how this could be done in a legal fashion" and there "was a sense that there was not an available mechanism to simply not spend money" that already had been notified to Congress or earmarked for Ukraine. Cooper Dep. Tr. at 47-48.

repeated requests to learn the reason for the hold.[90] Deputy Assistant Secretary of Defense Laura

Cooper, whose responsibilities include the Ukraine security assistance, testified that she had "no

recollection of the issue of allied burden sharing coming up" in the three meetings she attended

about the freeze on security assistance, nor did she recall hearing about a lack of funding from

Ukraine's allies as a reason for the freeze.[91] Ms. Cooper further testified that there was no policy or

interagency review process relating to the Ukraine security assistance that she "participated in or

knew of" in August 2019.[92] In addition, while the aid was being withheld, Ambassador Sondland,

the U.S. Ambassador to the EU, was never asked to reach out to the EU or its member states to ask

them to increase their contributions to Ukraine.[93]

45.   Two OMB career officials, including one of its legal counsel, ultimately resigned, in

part, over concerns about the handling of the hold on security assistance.[94] A confidential White

House review has reportedly "turned up hundreds of documents that reveal extensive efforts to

generate an after-the-fact justification" for the hold.[95]

46.   Throughout August, officials from DOD warned officials from OMB that, as the

hold continued, there was an increasing risk that the funds for Ukraine would not be timely

obligated, in violation of the Impoundment Control Act of 1974.[96] On January 16, 2020, the U.S.

---

[90] Sandy Dep. Tr. at 42-43.

[91] Cooper-Hale Hearing Tr. at 75-76.

[92] Cooper Dep. Tr. at 91.

[93] Sondland Dep. Tr. at 338-39.

[94] Sandy Dep. Tr. at 149-55.

[95] Josh Dawsey et al., *White House Review Turns Up Emails Showing Extensive Efforts to Justify Trump's Decision to Block Ukraine Military Aid*, Wash. Post (Nov. 24, 2019), https://perma.cc/99TX-5KFE. Because the President obstructed the House's investigation, the House was unable to obtain documents to confirm this reporting.

[96] *See* Sandy Dep. Tr. at 75; Kate Brannen, *Exclusive: Unredacted Ukraine Documents Reveal Extent of Pentagon's Legal Concerns*, Just Security (Jan. 2, 2020) (Just Security Report), https://perma.cc/VA6U-RYPK (reporting about review of unredacted copies of OMB documents that were produced to the Center for Public Integrity in redacted form).

Government Accountability Office (GAO) concluded that OMB had, in fact, violated the

Impoundment Control Act when it withheld from obligation funds appropriated by Congress to

DOD for security assistance to Ukraine. GAO stated that "[f]aithful execution of the law does not

permit the President to substitute his own policy priorities for those that Congress has enacted into

law."[97]

47. In late August, Secretary of Defense Mike Esper, Secretary of State Pompeo, and

National Security Advisor Bolton reportedly urged the President to release the aid to Ukraine,

advising the President that the aid was in America's national security interest.[98] On August 30,

however, an OMB official advised a Pentagon official by email that there was a "clear direction from

POTUS to continue to hold."[99]

48. Contrary to U.S. national security interests—and over the objections of his own

advisors—President Trump continued to withhold the funding to Ukraine through August and into

September, without any credible explanation.[100]

D. President Trump Conditioned a White House Meeting on Ukraine Announcing It Would Launch Politically Motivated Investigations

49. Upon his arrival in Kyiv in June 2019, Ambassador Taylor sought to schedule the

promised White House meeting for President Zelensky, which was "an agreed-upon goal" of

policymakers in Ukraine and the United States.[101]

---

[97] Matter of Office of Mgmt. & Budget—Withholding of Ukraine Sec. Assistance, B-331564 (Comp. Gen. Jan. 16, 2020), https://perma.cc/5CDX-XLX6.

[98] *See Behind the Ukraine Aid Freeze*, https://perma.cc/TA5J-NJFX.

[99] *See* Just Security Report, https://perma.cc/VA6U-RYPK (quoting email from Michael Duffey to Elaine McCusker).

[100] *See, e.g.*, Sandy Dep. Tr. at 133 ("[W]ere we ever given any reason for the hold? And I would say only in September did we receive an explanation that the hold—that the President's direction reflected his concerns about the contributions from other countries for Ukraine."); Cooper Dep. Tr. at 93-94; Vindman Dep. Tr. at 181-82; Williams Dep. at 91-92.

[101] Taylor Dep. Tr. at 24-25 ("In late June, one of the goals of both channels was to facilitate a visit by President Zelensky to the White House for a meeting with President Trump, which

50.   As Ambassador Volker explained, a White House visit by President Zelensky would constitute "a tremendous symbol of support" for Ukraine and would "enhance[] [President Zelensky's] stature."[102]

51.   Ambassador Taylor learned, however, that President Trump "wanted to hear from Zelensky," who had to "make clear" to President Trump that he was not "standing in the way of 'investigations.'"[103] It soon became clear to Ambassador Taylor and others that the White House meeting would not be scheduled until the Ukraine committed to the investigations of "Burisma and alleged Ukrainian influence in the 2016 elections."[104]

52.   Ambassador Sondland was unequivocal in describing this conditionality. He testified:

> I know that members of this committee frequently frame these complicated issues in the form of a simple question: Was there a quid pro quo? As I testified previously with regard to the requested White House call and the White House meeting, the answer is yes.[105]

53.   According to Ambassador Sondland, the public *announcement* of the investigations— and not necessarily the pursuit of the investigations themselves—was the price President Trump sought in exchange for a White House meeting with Ukrainian President Zelensky.[106]

54.   Both Ambassadors Volker and Sondland explicitly communicated this quid pro quo to Ukrainian government officials. For example, on July 2, in Toronto, Canada, Ambassador Volker

---

President Trump had promised in his congratulatory letter of May 29. [The] Ukrainians were clearly eager for the meeting to happen. During a conference call with Ambassador Volker, Acting Assistant Secretary of State for European and Eurasian Affairs Phil Reeker, Secretary Perry, Ambassador Sondland, and Counselor of the U.S. Department of State Ulrich Brechbuhl on June 18, it was clear that a meeting between the two presidents was an agreed-on—agreed-upon goal.").

[102] Volker Interview Tr. at 59, 328.
[103] *Id.*
[104] Taylor Dep. Tr. at 26.
[105] Sondland Hearing Tr. at 26.
[106] *Id.* at 43.

conveyed the message directly to President Zelensky and referred to the "Giuliani factor" in President Zelensky's engagement with the United States.[107] Ambassador Volker told Ambassador Taylor that during the Toronto conference, he counseled President Zelensky about how he "could prepare for the phone call with President Trump"—specifically, that President Trump "would like to hear about the investigations."[108]

55.   Ambassador Volker confirmed that, in "a pull-aside" meeting in Toronto, he "advise[d] [President Zelensky] that he should call President Trump personally because he needed to . . . be able to convey to President Trump that he was serious about fighting corruption, investigating things that happened in the past and so forth."[109] Upon hearing about this discussion, Deputy Assistant Secretary of State for European and Eurasian Affairs George Kent told Ambassador Volker that "asking for another country to investigate a prosecution for political reasons undermines our advocacy of the rule of law."[110]

56.   On July 10, at a meeting with Ukrainian officials in Ambassador Bolton's office at the White House, Ambassador Sondland was even more explicit about the quid pro quo. He stated—in front of multiple witnesses, including two top advisors to President Zelensky and Ambassador Bolton—that he had an arrangement with Mr. Mulvaney to schedule the White House visit after Ukraine initiated the "investigations."[111]

57.   In a second meeting in the White House Ward Room shortly thereafter, "Ambassador Sondland, in front of the Ukrainians . . . was talking about how he had an agreement with Chief of Staff Mulvaney for a meeting with the Ukrainians if they were going to go forward

---

[107] Kurt Volker Text Messages Received by the House Committees at KV00000027 (Oct. 2, 2019) (Volker Text Messages), https://perma.cc/CG7Y-FHXZ.
[108] Taylor Dep. Tr. at 65-66.
[109] Volker-Morrison Hearing Tr. at 70.
[110] Kent Dep. Tr. at 246-47.
[111] Hill Dep. Tr. at 67.

with investigations."[112] More specifically, Lt. Col. Vindman testified that Ambassador Sondland said "[t]hat the Ukrainians would have to deliver an investigation into the Bidens."[113]

58.   During that meeting, Dr. Hill and Lt. Col. Vindman objected to Ambassador Sondland intertwining what Dr. Hill later described as a "domestic political errand" with official national security policy toward Ukraine.[114]

59.   Following the July 10 meetings, Dr. Hill discussed what had occurred with Ambassador Bolton, including Ambassador Sondland's reiteration of the quid pro quo to the Ukrainians in the Ward Room. Ambassador Bolton told her to "go and tell [the NSC Legal Advisor] that I am not part of whatever drug deal Sondland and Mulvaney are cooking up on this."[115]

60.   Both Dr. Hill and Lt. Col. Vindman separately reported Sondland's description of the quid pro quo during the July 10 meetings to NSC Legal Advisor, John Eisenberg, who said he would follow up.[116]

61.   After the July 10 meetings, Andriy Yermak, a top aide to President Zelensky who was in the meetings, followed up with Ambassador Volker by text message: "Thank you for

---

[112] *Id.* at 69.

[113] Vindman Dep. Tr. at 64.

[114] *Id.* at 69-70; Vindman Dep. Tr. at 31; *see* Hill-Holmes Hearing Tr. at 92.

[115] Hill Dep. Tr. at 70-72.

[116] *Id.* at 139 ("I told him exactly, you know, what had transpired and that Ambassador Sondland had basically indicated that there was an agreement with the Chief of Staff that they would have a White House meeting or, you know, a Presidential meeting if the Ukrainians started up these investigations again."); Vindman Dep. Tr. at 37 ("Sir, I think I—I mean, the top line I just offered, I'll restate it, which is that Mr. Sondland asked for investigations, for these investigations into Bidens and Burisma. I actually recall having that particular conversation. Mr. Eisenberg doesn't really work on this issue, so I had to go a little bit into the back story of what these investigations were, and that I expressed concerns and thought it was inappropriate."). A third NSC official, P. Wells Griffith, also reported the July 10 meeting to the NSC Legal Advisor, but he refused to comply with a subpoena and did not testify before the House.

meeting and your clear and very logical position . . . I feel that the key for many things is Rudi [*sic*] and I [am] ready to talk with him at any time."[117]

62.   Over the next two weeks, Ambassadors Sondland and Volker coordinated with Mr. Giuliani and senior Ukrainian and American officials to arrange a telephone call between President Trump and President Zelensky. They also worked to ensure that, during that phone call, President Zelensky would convince President Trump of his willingness to undertake the investigations in order to get the White House meeting scheduled.[118]

63.   On July 19, Ambassador Volker had breakfast with Mr. Giuliani at the Trump Hotel in Washington, D.C. After the meeting, Ambassador Volker reported back to Ambassadors Sondland and Taylor about his conversation with Mr. Giuliani, stating, "Most impt is for Zelensky to say that he will help investigation—and address any specific personnel issues—if there are any."[119]

64.   The same day, Ambassador Sondland spoke with President Zelensky and recommended that the Ukrainian leader tell President Trump that he "will leave no stone unturned" regarding the investigations during the upcoming Presidential phone call.[120]

65.   Following his conversation with President Zelensky, Ambassador Sondland emailed top Trump Administration officials, including Secretary Pompeo, Mr. Mulvaney, and Secretary Perry. Ambassador Sondland stated that President Zelensky confirmed that he would "assure"

---

[117] Volker Text Messages at KV00000018.

[118] *See, e.g., id.* at KV00000037; Ambassador Gordon D. Sondland, *Opening Statement Before the U.S. House of Representatives Permanent Select Comm. on Intelligence* 15 (Nov. 20, 2019) (Sondland Opening Statement), https://perma.cc/Z2W6-A9HS ("As I communicated to the team, I told President Zelensky in advance that assurances to run a fully transparent investigation and turn over every stone were necessary in his call with President Trump.").

[119] Volker Text Messages at KV00000037.

[120] Taylor-Kent Hearing Tr. at 37-38 (Ambassador Taylor quoting Ambassador Sondland).

President Trump that "he intends to run a fully transparent investigation and will 'turn over every stone.'"[121]

66.   Secretary Perry responded to Ambassador Sondland's email, "Mick just confirmed the call being set up for tomorrow by NSC." About an hour later, Mr. Mulvaney replied, "I asked NSC to set it up for tomorrow."[122]

67.   According to Ambassador Sondland, this email—and other correspondence with top Trump Administration officials—showed that his efforts regarding Ukraine were not part of a rogue foreign policy. To the contrary, Ambassador Sondland testified that "everyone was in the loop."[123]

68.   The Ukrainians also understood the quid pro quo—and the domestic U.S. political ramifications of the investigations they were being asked to pursue. On July 20, a close advisor to President Zelensky warned Ambassador Taylor that the Ukrainian leader "did not want to be used as a pawn in a U.S. reelection campaign."[124] The next day, Ambassador Taylor warned Ambassador Sondland that President Zelensky was "sensitive about Ukraine being taken seriously, not merely as an instrument in Washington domestic, reelection politics."[125]

69.   Nevertheless, President Trump, directly and through his hand-picked representatives, continued to press the Ukrainian government for the announcement of the investigations, including during President Trump's July 25 call with President Zelensky.[126]

---

[121] Sondland Hearing Tr. at 27; Sondland Opening Statement at 21, Ex. 4.
[122] Sondland Opening Statement at 21, Ex. 4.
[123] Sondland Hearing Tr. at 27.
[124] Taylor Dep. Tr. at 30.
[125] Volker Text Messages at KV00000037.
[126] *See, e.g., id.* at KV00000019; July 25 Memorandum at 3-4, https://perma.cc/8JRD-6K9V.

E. President Trump Directly Solicited Election Interference from President Zelensky

70.   In the days leading up to President Trump's July 25 call with President Zelensky, U.S. polling data showed former Vice President Biden leading in a head-to-head contest against President Trump.[127]

71.   Meanwhile, Ambassadors Sondland and Volker continued to prepare President Zelensky and his advisors for the call with President Trump until right before it occurred.

72.   On the morning of July 25, Ambassador Sondland spoke with President Trump in advance of his call with President Zelensky. Ambassador Sondland then called Ambassador Volker and left a voicemail.[128]

73.   After receiving Ambassador Sondland's message, Ambassador Volker sent a text message to President Zelensky's aide, Mr. Yermak, approximately 30 minutes before the call:

> Heard from White House—assuming President Z convinces trump he
> will investigate / "get to the bottom of what happened" in 2016, we
> will nail down date for visit to Washington. Good luck![129]

74.   In his public testimony, Ambassador Sondland confirmed that Ambassador Volker's text message to Mr. Yermak accurately summarized the directive he had received from President Trump earlier that morning.[130]

75.   During the roughly 30-minute July 25 call, President Zelensky thanked President Trump for the "great support in the area of defense" provided by the United States and stated that Ukraine would soon be prepared to purchase additional Javelin anti-tank missiles from the United States.[131]

---

[127] *See, e.g., Washington Post–ABC News Poll, June 28–July 1, 2019,* Wash. Post (July 11, 2019), https://perma.cc/NS4B-PRWC.

[128] Sondland Hearing Tr. at 53-54.

[129] Volker Text Messages at KV00000019.

[130] Sondland Hearing Tr. at 53-55.

[131] *See* July 25 Memorandum at 2, https://perma.cc/8JRD-6K9V.

76.   President Trump immediately responded with his own request: "I would like you to do us a favor though," which was "to find out what happened" with alleged Ukrainian interference in the 2016 election and to "look into" former Vice President Biden's role in encouraging the removal of the former Ukrainian prosecutor general.

77.   Referencing Special Counsel Mueller's investigation into Russian interference in the 2016 election, President Trump told President Zelensky, "[T]hey say a lot of it started with Ukraine," and "[w]hatever you can do, it's very important that you do it if that's possible."[132]

78.   President Trump repeatedly pressed the Ukrainian President to consult with his personal lawyer, Mr. Giuliani, as well as Attorney General William Barr, about the two specific investigations.[133] President Trump stated, "Rudy very much knows what's happening and he is a very capable guy. If you could speak to him that would be great."[134]

79.   President Zelensky agreed, referencing Mr. Giuliani's back-channel role, noting that Mr. Yermak "spoke with Mr. Giuliani just recently and we are hoping very much that Mr. Giuliani will be able to travel to Ukraine and we will meet once he comes to Ukraine."[135]

80.   Later in the call, President Zelensky heeded the directives he had received from Ambassadors Sondland and Volker: he thanked President Trump for his invitation to the White House and then reiterated that, "[o]n the other hand," he would "ensure" that Ukraine pursued "the

---

[132] *Id.* at 3-4. President Trump continues to embrace this call as both "routine" and "perfect." *See, e.g., Remarks by President Trump upon Arriving at the U.N. General Assembly*, White House (Sept. 24, 2019) (Trump Sept. 24 Remarks), https://perma.cc/ZQ4P-FGT4; Colby Itkowitz, *Trump Defends Call with Ukrainian President, Calling It "Perfectly Fine and Routine,"* Wash. Post (Sept. 21, 2019), https://perma.cc/T3ZM-GKLB.

[133] *See* July 25 Memorandum at 4-5, https://perma.cc/8JRD-6K9V.

[134] *Id.* at 4.

[135] *Id.*

investigation" that President Trump had requested. President Zelensky confirmed the investigations should be done "openly."[136]

81.   During the call, President Trump also attacked Ambassador Yovanovitch. He said, "The former ambassador from the United States, the woman, was bad news and the people she was dealing with in the Ukraine were bad news so I just want to let you know that." He later added, "Well, she's going to go through some things." President Trump also defended then-Ukrainian Prosecutor General Yuriy Lutsenko, who was widely known to be corrupt.[137]

82.   The President did not mention any other issues relating to Ukraine, including concerns about Ukrainian corruption, President Zelensky's anti-corruption reforms, or the ongoing war with Russia. The President only identified two people in reference to investigations: Vice President Biden and his son.[138]

83.   Listening to the call as it transpired, several White House staff members became alarmed. Lt. Col. Vindman immediately reported his concerns to NSC lawyers because, as he testified, "[i]t is improper for the President of the United States to demand a foreign government investigate a U.S. citizen and a political opponent."[139]

84.   Jennifer Williams, an advisor to Vice President Pence, testified that the call struck her as "unusual and inappropriate" and that "the references to specific individuals and investigations, such as former Vice President Biden and his son, struck me as political in nature."[140]

---

[136] *Id.* at 3, 5.

[137] *See id.* at 2.

[138] *See generally id.* Mr. Trump had previously engaged in efforts to cut aid to anti-corruption programs in Ukraine and other foreign nations. *See* Erica Werner, *Trump Administration Sought Billions of Dollars in Cuts to Programs Aimed at Fighting Corruption in Ukraine and Elsewhere*, Wash. Post (Oct. 23, 2019), https://perma.cc/R9AJ-AZ65.

[139] Transcript, *Impeachment Inquiry: Ms. Jennifer Williams and Lieutenant Colonel Alexander Vindman: Hearing Before the H. Permanent Select Comm. on Intelligence*, 116th Cong. 19 (Nov. 19, 2019) (Vindman-Williams Hearing Tr.).

[140] *Id.* at 34; Williams Dep. Tr. at 148-49.

She believed President Trump's solicitation of an investigation was "inappropriate" because it "appeared to be a domestic political matter."[141]

85.   Timothy Morrison, Dr. Hill's successor as the NSC's Senior Director for Europe and Russia and Lt. Col. Vindman's supervisor, said that "the call was not the full-throated endorsement of the Ukraine reform agenda that I was hoping to hear."[142] He too reported the call to NSC lawyers, worrying that the call would be "damaging" if leaked publicly.[143]

86.   In response, Mr. Eisenberg and his deputy, Michael Ellis, tightly restricted access to the call summary, which was placed on a highly classified NSC server even though it did not contain any highly classified information.[144]

87.   On July 26, the day after the call, Ambassador Sondland had lunch with State Department aides in Kyiv, including David Holmes, the Counselor for Political Affairs at the U.S. Embassy in Kyiv. During the lunch, Ambassador Sondland called President Trump directly from his cellphone. President Trump asked Ambassador Sondland whether President Zelensky was "going to do the investigation." Ambassador Sondland stated that President Zelensky was "going to do it" and would "do anything you ask him to."[145]

88.   After the call, it was clear to Ambassador Sondland that "a public statement from President Zelensky" committing to the investigations was a "prerequisite" for a White House meeting.[146] He told Mr. Holmes that President Trump "did not give a [expletive] about Ukraine." Rather, the President cared only about "big stuff" that benefited him personally, like "the Biden

---

141 Vindman-Williams Hearing Tr. at 15.
142 Morrison Dep. Tr. at 41.
143 *Id.* at 43.
144 *Id.* at 43, 47-50, 52; *see also* Vindman Dep. Tr. at 49-51, 119-22.
145 Holmes Dep. Tr. at 24.
146 Sondland Hearing Tr. at 26-27.

investigation that Mr. Giuliani was pushing," and that President Trump had directly solicited during the July 25 call.[147]

F. President Trump Conditioned the Release of Security Assistance for Ukraine, and Continued to Leverage a White House Meeting, to Pressure Ukraine to Launch Politically Motivated Investigations

89.   As discussed further below, following the July 25 call, President Trump's representatives, including Ambassadors Sondland and Volker, in coordination with Mr. Giuliani, pressed the Ukrainians to issue a public statement announcing the investigations. At the same time, officials in both the United States and Ukraine became increasingly concerned about President Trump's continuing hold on security assistance.[148]

90.   The Ukrainian government was aware of the hold by at least late July, around the time of President Trump's July 25 call with President Zelensky. On the day of the call itself, DOD officials learned that diplomats at the Ukrainian Embassy in Washington, D.C., had made multiple overtures to DOD and the State Department "asking about security assistance."[149]

91.   Around this time, two different officials at the Ukrainian Embassy approached Ambassador Volker's special advisor to ask her about the hold.[150]

92.   By mid-August, before the hold was public, Lt. Col. Vindman also received inquiries from the Ukrainian Embassy. Lt. Col. Vindman testified that during this timeframe, "it was no secret, at least within government and official channels, that security assistance was on hold."[151]

93.   The former Ukrainian deputy foreign minister, Olena Zerkal, has acknowledged that she became aware of the hold on security assistance no later than July 30 based on a diplomatic

---

[147] Holmes Dep. Tr. at 25-26.

[148] *See, e.g.,* Cooper-Hale Hearing Tr. at 13-14; Vindman Dep. Tr. at 222; Sandy Dep. Tr. at 59-60.

[149] Cooper-Hale Hearing Tr. at 13-14.

[150] Croft Dep. Tr. at 86-88.

[151] Vindman Dep. Tr. at 222.

cable—transmitted the previous week—from Ukrainian officials in Washington, D.C.[152] She said that President Zelensky's office had received a copy of the cable "simultaneously."[153] Ms. Zerkal further stated that President Zelensky's top advisor, Andriy Yermak, told her "to keep silent, to not comment without permission" about the hold or about when the Ukrainian government became aware of it.[154]

94.   In early August, Ambassadors Sondland and Volker, in coordination with Mr. Giuliani, endeavored to pressure President Zelensky to make a public statement announcing the investigations. On August 10—in a text message that showed the Ukrainians' understanding of the quid pro quo—President Zelensky's advisor, Mr. Yermak, told Ambassador Volker that, once a date was set for the White House meeting, he would "call for a press briefing, announcing upcoming visit and outlining vision for the reboot of US-UKRAINE relationship, including among other things Burisma and election meddling in investigations[.]"[155]

95.   On August 11, Ambassador Sondland emailed two State Department officials, one of whom acted as a direct line to Secretary Pompeo, to inform them about the agreement for President Zelensky to issue a statement that would include an announcement of the two investigations. Ambassador Sondland stated that he expected a draft of the statement to be "delivered for our review in a day or two[,]" and that he hoped the statement would "make the boss [i.e., President Trump] happy enough to authorize an invitation" for a White House meeting.[156]

96.   On August 12, Mr. Yermak texted Ambassador Volker an initial draft of the statement. The draft referred to "the problem of interference in the political processes of the

---

[152] Andrew E. Kramer, *Ukraine Knew of Aid Freeze in July, Says Ex-Top Official in Kyiv*, N.Y. Times (Dec. 3, 2019), https://perma.cc/SD98-VPRN.

[153] *Id.* (quoting Ms. Zerkal).

[154] *Id.* (quoting Ms. Zerkal's summary of a statement by Mr. Yermak).

[155] Volker Text Messages at KV00000019.

[156] Sondland Opening Statement at 22, Ex. 7; Sondland Hearing Tr. at 28, 102.

United States," but it did not explicitly mention the two investigations that President Trump had requested in the July 25 call.[157]

97.   The next day, Ambassadors Volker and Sondland discussed the draft statement with Mr. Giuliani, who told them, "If [the statement] doesn't say Burisma and 2016, it's not credible[.]"[158] As Ambassador Sondland would later testify, "Mr. Giuliani was expressing the desires of the President of the United States, and we knew these investigations were important to the President."[159]

98.   Ambassadors Volker and Sondland relayed this message to Mr. Yermak and sent him a revised statement that included explicit references to "Burisma and the 2016 U.S. elections."[160]

99.   In light of President Zelensky's anti-corruption agenda, Ukrainian officials resisted issuing the statement in August and, as a result, there was no movement toward scheduling the White House meeting.[161]

100.   Meanwhile, there was growing concern about President Trump's continued hold on the security assistance for Ukraine. The hold remained in place through August, against the unanimous judgment of American national security officials charged with overseeing U.S.-Ukraine policy. For example, during a high-level interagency meeting in late July, officials unanimously advocated for releasing the hold—with the sole exception of OMB, which was acting under

---

[157] Volker Text Messages at KV00000020.

[158] Volker Interview Tr. at 113.

[159] Sondland Hearing Tr. at 18.

[160] Volker Text Messages at KV00000023. Ambassador Volker claimed that he "stopped pursuing" the statement from the Ukrainians around this time because of concerns raised by Mr. Yermak. Ambassador Kurt Volker, *Testimony Before the House of Representatives Committee on Foreign Affairs, Permanent Select Committee on Intelligence, and Committee on Oversight* 8 (Oct. 3, 2019) (Volker Opening Statement), https://perma.cc/9DDN-2WFW; Volker Interview Tr. at 44-45, 199; Volker-Morrison Hearing Tr. at 21.

[161] *See, e.g.*, Sondland Opening Statement at 16 ("[M]y goal, at the time, was to do what was necessary to get the aid released, to break the logjam. I believed that the public statement we had been discussing for weeks was essential to advancing that goal.").

"guidance from the President and from Acting Chief of Staff Mulvaney to freeze the assistance."[162] But even officials within OMB had internally recommended that the hold be removed because "assistance to Ukraine is consistent with [U.S.] national security strategy," provides the "benefit . . . of opposing Russian aggression," and is backed by "bipartisan support."[163]

101.   Without an explanation for the hold, and with President Trump already conditioning a White House visit on the announcement of the investigations, it became increasingly apparent to multiple witnesses that the security assistance was being withheld in order to pressure Ukraine to announce the investigations. As Ambassador Sondland testified, President Trump's effort to condition release of the security assistance on an announcement of the investigations was as clear as "two plus two equals four."[164]

102.   On August 22, Ambassador Sondland emailed Secretary Pompeo in an effort to "break the logjam" on the security assistance and the White House meeting. He proposed that President Trump should arrange to speak to President Zelensky during an upcoming trip to Warsaw, during which President Zelensky could "look [President Trump] in the eye and tell him" he was prepared "to move forward publicly . . . on those issues of importance to Potus and to the U.S."— i.e., the announcement of the two investigations.[165]

103.   On August 28, news of the hold was publicly reported by *Politico*.[166]

---

[162] Hale Dep. Tr. at 81; Vindman Dep. Tr. at 184.

[163] Sandy Dep. Tr. at 59-60.

[164] Sondland Hearing Tr. at 56-58; *see also* Taylor Dep. Tr. at 190 (Ambassador Taylor's "clear understanding" was that "security assistance money would not come until the [Ukrainian] President committed to pursue the investigation"); Hill-Holmes Hearing Tr. at 32 (Mr. Holmes's "clear impression was that the security assistance hold was likely intended by the President either as an expression of dissatisfaction with the Ukrainians, who had not yet agreed to the Burisma/Biden investigation, or as an effort to increase the pressure on them to do so.").

[165] Sondland Opening Statement at 23.

[166] Caitlin Emma & Connor O'Brien, *Trump Holds Up Ukraine Military Aid Meant to Confront Russia*, Politico (Aug. 28, 2019), https://perma.cc/54RZ-Q6NJ.

104.   As soon as the hold became public, Ukrainian officials expressed significant concern to U.S. officials.[167] They were deeply worried not only about the practical impact that the hold would have on efforts to fight Russian aggression, but also about the symbolic message the now-publicized lack of support from the Trump Administration sent to the Russian government, which would almost certainly seek to exploit any real or perceived crack in U.S. resolve toward Ukraine. Mr. Yermak and other Ukrainian officials told Ambassador Taylor that they were "desperate" and would be willing to travel to Washington to raise with U.S. officials the importance of the assistance.[168] The recently appointed Ukrainian prosecutor general later remarked, "It's critically important for the west not to pull us into some conflicts between their ruling elites[.]"[169]

105.   On September 1—within days of President Trump rejecting the request from Secretaries Pompeo and Esper and Ambassador Bolton to release the hold[170]—Vice President Pence met with President Zelensky in Warsaw, Poland after President Trump cancelled his trip.[171]

106.   In advance of this meeting, Ambassador Sondland told Vice President Pence that he "had concerns that the delay in aid had become tied to the issue of investigations."[172] Sondland testified that Vice President Pence "nodded like, you know, he heard what I said, and that was pretty much it."[173]

---

[167] Volker Text Messages at KV00000020; Volker Interview Tr. at 80-81; Taylor Dep. Tr. at 34.

[168] Taylor Dep. Tr. at 137-38.

[169] Roman Olearchyk, *Cleaning Up Ukraine in the Shadow of Trump*, Fin. Times (Nov. 28, 2019), https://perma.cc/YMX9-XJ2B (quoting current Ukrainian Prosecutor General Ruslan Ryaboshapka).

[170] *Behind the Ukraine Aid Freeze*, https://perma.cc/TA5J-NJFX.

[171] *Readout of Vice President Mike Pence's Meeting with Ukrainian President Volodymyr Zelenskyy*, White House (Sep. 1, 2019), https://perma.cc/K2PH-YPVK; Taylor-Kent Hearing Tr. at 41.

[172] Sondland Hearing Tr. at 30.

[173] *Id.* at 38.

107.   During the meeting that followed, which Ambassador Sondland also attended, "the very first question" that President Zelensky asked Vice President Pence related to the status of U.S. security assistance.[174] President Zelensky emphasized that "the symbolic value of U.S. support in terms of security assistance . . . was just as valuable to the Ukrainians as the actual dollars."[175] He also voiced concern that "any hold or appearance of reconsideration of such assistance might embolden Russia to think that the United States was no longer committed to Ukraine."[176]

108.   Vice President Pence told President Zelensky that he would speak with President Trump that evening. Although Vice President Pence did speak with President Trump, the President still did not lift the hold.[177]

109.   Following the meeting between Vice President Pence and President Zelensky, Ambassador Sondland pulled aside President Zelensky's advisor, Mr. Yermak, to explain that "the resumption of U.S. aid would likely not occur until Ukraine took some kind of action on [issuing a] public statement" about the investigations.[178]

110.   Immediately following that conversation, Ambassador Sondland walked over to Mr. Morrison, who had been standing across the room observing their interactions. Ambassador Sondland told Mr. Morrison that "what he had communicated [to Mr. Yermak] was that . . . what could help [Ukraine] move the aid was if the prosecutor general would go to the mike [*sic*] and announce that he was opening" the investigations.[179]

---

[174] Williams Dep. Tr. at 81.
[175] *Id.* at 82.
[176] *Id.* at 82-83.
[177] *Id.* at 94.
[178] Sondland Hearing Tr. at 31.
[179] Morrison Dep. Tr. at 134.

111.   Later that day, Mr. Morrison reported this conversation to Ambassador Bolton, who advised him to "stay out of it" and to brief the NSC's lawyers. Mr. Morrison subsequently reported the conversation to Mr. Eisenberg.[180]

112.   Mr. Morrison also informed Ambassador Taylor about his conversation with Ambassador Sondland. Ambassador Taylor was "alarmed by what Mr. Morrison told [him] about the Sondland-Yermak conversation."[181] He followed up by texting Ambassador Sondland, "Are we now saying that security assistance and WH meeting are conditioned on investigations?" Ambassador Sondland responded, "Call me."[182]

113.   Ambassadors Sondland and Taylor then spoke by telephone. Ambassador Sondland again relayed what he told Mr. Yermak and explained that he had made a "mistake" in telling Ukrainian officials that *only* the White House meeting was conditioned on a public announcement of the investigations. He clarified that "everything"—the White House meeting *and* security assistance for Ukraine—was conditioned on the announcement of the investigations.[183] Ambassador Sondland explained to Ambassador Taylor that "President Trump wanted President Zelensky in a public box, by making a public statement about ordering such investigations."[184]

114.   On September 7, President Trump and Ambassador Sondland spoke by telephone.[185] As Ambassador Sondland relayed later that day during a call with Mr. Morrison, President Trump

---

[180] *Id.* at 182-83.

[181] Taylor-Kent Hearing Tr. at 42.

[182] Volker Text Messages at KV00000039.

[183] Taylor-Kent Hearing Tr. at 42.

[184] *Id.*; *see also* Taylor Dep. Tr. at 144.

[185] In Ambassador Sondland's testimony, he was not clear on whether he had one or two conversations with the President in which the subject of a quid pro quo came up, or on precisely which date such conversations took place during the period of September 6 through 9. Regardless of the date, Ambassador Sondland did not contest telling both Mr. Morrison and Ambassador Taylor—both of whom took contemporaneous notes—of a conversation he had with the President that reaffirmed Ambassador Sondland's understanding that President Zelensky had to make a public statement announcing the investigations in order to obtain the White House meeting and security

told him "that there was no quid pro quo, but President Zelensky must announce the opening of the investigations and he should want to do it."[186]

115.   Mr. Morrison conveyed the substance of the September 7 call between President Trump and Ambassador Sondland to Ambassador Taylor. Mr. Morrison said that the call had given him "a sinking feeling" because he feared the security assistance would not be released before September 30, the end of the fiscal year, and because he "did not think it was a good idea for the Ukrainian President to . . . involve himself in our politics."[187] At Ambassador Bolton's direction, Mr. Morrison reported Ambassador Sondland's description of the President's statements to the NSC lawyers.[188]

116.   The next day, September 8, Ambassador Sondland confirmed in a phone call with Ambassador Taylor that he had spoken to President Trump and that "President Trump was adamant that President Zelensky himself had to" announce the investigations publicly.[189]

117.   Ambassador Sondland also told Ambassador Taylor that he had passed President Trump's message directly to President Zelensky and Mr. Yermak and had told them that "although this was not a quid pro quo, if President Zelensky did not clear things up in public, we would be at a stalemate"—meaning "Ukraine would not receive the much-needed military assistance."[190]

---

assistance. *See* Sondland Hearing Tr. at 109. Both documentary evidence and testimony confirmed that the conversation described by Mr. Morrison and Ambassador Taylor occurred on September 7. *See, e.g.*, Morrison Dep. Tr. at 144-45; Taylor Dep. Tr. at 38; Volker Text Messages at KV00000053 (Sondland text message to Volker and Taylor on September 8 stating, "Guys, multiple convos with Ze, Potus. Lets talk").

[186] Morrison Dep. Tr. at 190-91.

[187] *Id.* at 145.

[188] *Id.* at 223, 238.

[189] Taylor-Kent Hearing Tr. at 44.

[190] Sondland Hearing Tr. at 7; Taylor Dep. Tr. at 39.

118.   Early the next morning, on September 9, Ambassador Taylor texted Ambassadors Sondland and Volker: "As I said on the phone, I think it's crazy to withhold security assistance for help with a political campaign."[191]

119.   The Ukrainians succumbed to the pressure. In early September, President Zelensky agreed to do a televised interview, during which he would publicly announce the investigations. The Ukrainians made arrangements for the interview to occur on CNN later in September.[192]

120.   The White House subsequently confirmed that the release of the security assistance had been conditioned on Ukraine's announcement of the investigations. During a White House press conference on October 17, Acting Chief of Staff Mulvaney acknowledged that he had discussed security assistance with the President and that the President's decision to withhold it was directly tied to his desire that Ukraine investigate alleged Ukrainian interference in the 2016 U.S. election.[193]

121.   After a reporter attempted to clarify this explicit acknowledgement of a "quid pro quo," Mr. Mulvaney replied, "We do that all the time with foreign policy." He added, "I have news for everybody: get over it. There is going to be political influence in foreign policy."[194]

---

[191] Volker Text Messages at KV00000053.

[192] Sondland Hearing Tr. at 110-11; Andrew E. Kramer, *Ukraine's Zelensky Bowed to Trump's Demands until Luck Spared Him*, N.Y. Times (Nov. 7, 2019), https://perma.cc/A5JE-N25L; Fareed Zakaria, *Zelensky Planned to Announce Trump's "Quo" on My Show. Here's What Happened.*, Wash. Post (Nov. 14, 2019) (*Zelensky Planned to Announce Trump's "Quo"*), https://perma.cc/MMT7-D8XJ.

[193] *Press Briefing by Acting Chief of Staff Mick Mulvaney*, White House (Oct. 17, 2019) (Oct. 17 Briefing), https://perma.cc/Q45H-EMC7 ("Q. So the demand for an investigation into the Democrats was part of the reason that he ordered to withhold funding to Ukraine? MR. MULVANEY: The look back to what happened in 2016— Q. The investigation into Democrats. MR. MULVANEY: —certainly was part of the thing that he was worried about in corruption with that nation. And that is absolutely appropriate. Q. And withholding the funding? MR. MULVANEY: Yeah. Which ultimately, then, flowed.").

[194] *Id.*

122. Multiple foreign policy and national security officials testified that the pursuit of investigations into the Bidens and alleged Ukrainian interference in the 2016 election was not part of official U.S. policy.[195] Instead, as Dr. Hill described, these investigations were part of a "domestic political errand" of President Trump.[196] Mr. Kent further explained that urging Ukraine to engage in "selective politically associated investigations or prosecutions" undermines our longstanding efforts to promote the rule of law abroad.[197]

123. Ambassador Volker, in response to an inquiry from President Zelensky's advisor, Mr. Yermak, confirmed that the U.S. Department of Justice (DOJ) did not make an official request for Ukraine's assistance in these investigations.[198]

124. Within hours after the White House publicly released a record of the July 25 call, DOJ itself confirmed in a statement that no such request was ever made:

> The President has not spoken with the Attorney General about having Ukraine investigate anything related to former Vice President Biden or his son. The President has not asked the Attorney General to contact Ukraine—on this or any other matter. The Attorney General has not communicated with Ukraine—on this or any other subject.[199]

---

[195] Volker-Morrison Hearing Tr. at 146-47 (Mr. Morrison did not follow up on the President's request to "investigate the Bidens" because he "did not understand it as a policy objective"); Vindman-Williams Hearing Tr. at 119 (Mr. Vindman confirmed that he was not "aware of any written product" from the NSC suggesting that these investigations were "part of the official policy of the United States"); Taylor-Kent Hearing Tr. at 179 ("Mrs. Demings[:] Was Mr. Giuliani promoting U.S. national interests or policy in Ukraine . . . ? Ambassador Taylor[:] I don't think so, ma'am. . . . Mr. Kent[:] No, he was not.").

[196] Hill-Holmes Hearing Tr. at 92.

[197] Taylor-Kent Hearing Tr. at 24.

[198] Volker Interview Tr. at 197.

[199] Morgan Chalfant & Brett Samuels, *White House Memo Shows Trump Pressed Ukraine Leader to Look into Biden*, Hill (Sept. 25, 2019), https://perma.cc/5LHW-V4EB (quoting DOJ spokesperson Kerri Kupec).

G. President Trump Was Forced to Lift the Hold but Has Continued to Solicit Foreign Interference in the Upcoming Election

125.   As noted above, by early September 2019, President Zelensky had signaled his willingness to announce the two investigations to secure a White House meeting and the security assistance. He was scheduled to make the announcement during a CNN interview later in September, but other events intervened.[200]

126.   On September 9, the House Permanent Select Committee on Intelligence, the Committee on Oversight and Reform, and the Committee on Foreign Affairs announced a joint investigation into the scheme by President Trump "to improperly pressure the Ukrainian government to assist the President's bid for reelection."[201] The same day, the Committees sent document production and preservation requests to the White House and the State Department.[202]

127.   NSC staff members believed that the Congressional investigation "might have the effect of releasing the hold" on Ukraine military assistance, because it would have been "potentially politically challenging" to "justify that hold."[203]

128.   Later that day, the Inspector General of the Intelligence Community (ICIG) wrote to the Chairman and Ranking Member of the Intelligence Committee notifying them that a

---

[200] Taylor Dep. Tr. at 207-209; Taylor-Kent Hearing Tr. at 158 ("[A]s we've determined, as we've discussed here on September 11th, just before any CNN discussion or interview, the hold was released, the hold on the security assistance was released." (quoting Ambassador Taylor)).

[201] Press Release, House Permanent Select Comm. on Intelligence, Three House Committees Launch Wide-Ranging Investigation into Trump-Giuliani Ukraine Scheme (Sept. 9, 2019) (Sept. 9 Press Release), https://perma.cc/AX4Y-PWSH.

[202] Letter from Chairman Eliot L. Engel, House Comm. on Foreign Affairs, et al., to Pat A. Cipollone, Counsel to the President 3-4 (Sept. 9, 2019) (Sept. 9 Letter), https://perma.cc/R2GH-TZ9P; Letter from Chairman Eliot L. Engel, House Comm. on Foreign Affairs, et al., to Michael R. Pompeo, Sec'y, Dep't of State (Sept. 9, 2019), https://perma.cc/C4W4-UBTF.

[203] Vindman Dep. Tr. at 304.

whistleblower had filed a complaint on August 12 that the ICIG had determined to be both an "urgent concern" and "credible." The ICIG did not disclose the contents of the complaint.[204]

129.   The ICIG further stated that the Acting Director of National Intelligence (DNI) had taken the unprecedented step of withholding the whistleblower complaint from Congress.[205] It was later revealed that the Acting DNI had done so as a result of communications with the White House and the Department of Justice.[206] The next day, September 10, Chairman Schiff wrote to Acting DNI Joseph Maguire to express his concern about the Acting DNI's "unprecedented departure from past practice" in withholding the whistleblower complaint and observed that the "failure to transmit to the Committee an urgent and credible whistleblower complaint, as required by law, raises the prospect that an urgent matter of a serious nature is being purposefully concealed from the Committee."[207]

130.   The White House was aware of the contents of the whistleblower complaint since at least August 26, when the Acting DNI informed the White House Counsel's Office of the complaint.[208] White House Counsel Pat Cipollone and Mr. Eisenberg reportedly briefed President

---

[204] Letter from Michael K. Atkinson, Inspector Gen. of the Intelligence Community, to Chairman Adam Schiff, House Permanent Select Comm. on Intelligence, and Ranking Member Devin Nunes, House Permanent Select Comm. on Intelligence 2 (Sept. 9, 2019), https://perma.cc/K78N-SMRR.

[205] *Id.*

[206] Maguire Hearing Tr. at 14, 19-24.

[207] Letter from Chairman Adam B. Schiff, House Permanent Select Comm. on Intelligence, to Joseph Maguire, Acting Dir. of Nat'l Intelligence (Sept. 10, 2019), https://perma.cc/9X9V-G5ZN.

[208] Transcript, *Whistleblower Disclosure: Hearing Before the H. Permanent Select Comm. on Intelligence*, 116th Cong. 110 (Sept. 26, 209) (testimony of Joseph Maguire, Acting Dir., Nat'l Intelligence) (Maguire Hearing Tr.) ("Chairman Schiff, when I received the letter from Michael Atkinson on the 26th of August, he concurrently sent a letter to the Office of White House Counsel asking the White House counsel to control and keep any information that pertained to that phone call on the 25th.").

Trump on the whistleblower complaint in late August and discussed whether they had to give it to Congress.[209]

131. On September 11—two days after the ICIG notified Congress of the whistleblower complaint and the three House Committees announced their investigation—President Trump lifted the hold on security assistance. As with the implementation of the hold, no credible reason was provided for lifting the hold.[210] At the time of the release, there had been no discernible changes in international assistance commitments for Ukraine or Ukrainian anti-corruption reforms.[211]

132. Because of the hold the President placed on security assistance for Ukraine, DOD was unable to spend approximately $35 million—or 14 percent—of the funds appropriated by Congress for fiscal year 2019.[212]

133. Congress was forced to pass a new law to extend the funding in order to ensure the full amount could be used by Ukraine to defend itself.[213] Still, by early December 2019, Ukraine had not received approximately $20 million of the military assistance.[214]

[209] Michael S. Schmidt et al., *Trump Knew of Whistle-Blower Complaint When He Released Aid to Ukraine*, N.Y. Times (Nov. 26, 2019), https://perma.cc/7473-YFSY.

[210] *See* Morgan Philips, *Trump Administration Lifts Hold on $250M in Military Aid for Ukraine*, Fox News (Sept. 12, 2019), https://perma.cc/8ABM-XNPV.

[211] *See, e.g.*, Morrison Dep. Tr. at 244; Vindman Dep. Tr. at 306; Williams Dep. Tr. at 147. Mr. Sandy testified that he was not aware of any other countries committing to provide more financial assistance to Ukraine prior to the lifting of the hold on September 11. Sandy Dep. Tr. at 180. Lt. Col. Vindman similarly confirmed that none of the "facts on the ground" changed before the President lifted the hold. Vindman Dep. Tr. at 306.

[212] Sandy Dep. Tr. at 146-47; H. Rep. No. 116-335, at 474.

[213] Continuing Appropriations Act, 2020, and Health Extenders Act of 2019, Pub. L. No. 116-59, § 124 (2019).

[214] Molly O'Toole & Sarah D. Wire, *Millions in Military Aid at Center of Impeachment Hasn't Reached Ukraine*, L.A. Times (Dec. 12, 2019), https://perma.cc/AR26-3KY2 (citing a DOD aide).

134.   Although the hold was lifted, the White House still had not announced a date for President Zelensky's meeting with President Trump, and there were indications that President Zelensky's interview with CNN would still occur.[215]

135.   On September 18, a week before President Trump was scheduled to meet with President Zelensky on the sidelines of the U.N. General Assembly in New York, Vice President Pence had a telephone call with President Zelensky. During the call, Vice President Pence "ask[ed] a bit more about . . . how Zelensky's efforts were going."[216] Additional details about this call were provided to the House by Vice President Pence's advisor, Jennifer Williams, but were classified by the Office of the Vice President.[217] Despite repeated requests, the Vice President has refused to declassify Ms. Williams' supplemental testimony.

136.   On September 18 or 19, at the urging of Ambassador Taylor,[218] President Zelensky cancelled the CNN interview.[219]

137.   To date, almost nine months after the initial invitation was extended by President Trump on April 21, a White House meeting for President Zelensky has not occurred.[220] Since the initial invitation, President Trump has met with more than a dozen world leaders at the White

---

[215] Hill-Holmes Hearing Tr. at 33; Taylor-Kent Hearing Tr. at 106-07; *see also Zelensky Planned to Announce Trump's "Quo"*, https://perma.cc/MMT7-D8XJ.

[216] Williams Dep. Tr. at 156.

[217] Classified Supp'l Submission of Jennifer Williams to the House Permanent Select Comm. on Intelligence (Nov. 26, 2019) (describing additional details of the Vice President's call with President Zelensky on September 18).

[218] Taylor-Kent Hearing Tr. at 106-07; Hill-Holmes Hearing Tr. at 33.

[219] *Zelensky Planned to Announce Trump's "Quo"*, https://perma.cc/MMT7-D8XJ.

[220] Hill-Holmes Hearing Tr. at 46-47 (testimony of David Holmes) ("And although the hold on the security assistance may have been lifted, there were still things they wanted that they weren't getting, including a meeting with the President in the Oval Office. . . . And I think that continues to this day.").

House, including a meeting in the Oval Office with the Foreign Minister of Russia on December 10.[221]

138.   Since lifting the hold, and even after the House impeachment inquiry was announced on September 24, President Trump has continued to press Ukraine to investigate Vice President Biden and alleged 2016 election interference by Ukraine.[222]

139.   On September 24, in remarks at the opening session of the U.N. General Assembly, President Trump stated: "What Joe Biden did for his son, that's something they [Ukraine] should be looking at."[223]

140.   On September 25, in a joint public press availability with President Zelensky, President Trump stated that "I want him to do whatever he can" in reference to the investigation of the Bidens.[224] The same day, President Trump denied that his pursuit of the investigation involved a quid pro quo.[225]

141.   On September 30, during remarks at the swearing-in of the new Labor Secretary, President Trump stated: "Now, the new President of Ukraine ran on the basis of no corruption. . . . But there was a lot of corruption having to do with the 2016 election against us. And we want to get to the bottom of it, and it's very important that we do."[226]

---

[221] John Hudson & Anne Gearan, *Trump Meets Russia's Top Diplomat amid Scrap over Election Interference*, Wash. Post (Dec. 10, 2019), https://perma.cc/X5WC-LKT5; *see also* Philip Bump, *Trump Promised Zelensky a White House Meeting. More Than a Dozen Other Leaders Got One Instead*, Wash. Post (Dec. 13, 2019), https://perma.cc/4XSP-R3JB (compiling White House meetings involving foreign officials since April 2019).

[222] *E.g.*, H. Rep. No. 116-346, at 124; *see also* Hill-Holmes Hearing Tr. at 46-47.

[223] Trump Sept. 24 Remarks, https://perma.cc/ZQ4P-FGT4.

[224] *Remarks by President Trump and President Zelensky of Ukraine Before Bilateral Meeting*, White House (Sept. 25, 2019) (Trump Sept. 25 Remarks), https://perma.cc/XCJ4-A67L.

[225] *Trump Quotes Sondland Quoting Him: "I Want Nothing. I Want No Quid Pro Quo.,"* CBS News (Nov. 20, 2019), https://perma.cc/X34R-QG3R.

[226] *Remarks by President Trump at the Swearing-In Ceremony of Secretary of Labor Eugene Scalia*, White House (Sept. 30, 2019) (Trump Sept. 30 Remarks), https://perma.cc/R94C-5HAY.

142.   On October 3, when asked by a reporter what he had hoped President Zelensky would do following their July 25 call, President Trump responded: "Well, I would think that, if they were honest about it, they'd start a major investigation into the Bidens. It's a very simple answer."[227] The President also suggested that "China should start an investigation into the Bidens, because what happened in China is just about as bad as what happened with—with Ukraine.[228]

143.   On October 4, President Trump equated his interest in "looking for corruption" to the investigation of two particular subjects: the Bidens and alleged Ukrainian interference in the 2016 election. He told reporters:

> What I want to do—and I think I have an obligation to do it, probably a duty to do it: corruption—we are looking for corruption. When you look at what Biden and his son did, and when you look at other people—what they've done. And I believe there was tremendous corruption with Biden, but I think there was beyond—I mean, beyond corruption—having to do with the 2016 campaign, and what these lowlifes did to so many people, to hurt so many people in the Trump campaign—which was successful, despite all of the fighting us. I mean, despite all of the unfairness.[229]

When asked by a reporter, "Is someone advising you that it is okay to solicit the help of other governments to investigate a potential political opponent?," Trump replied in part, "Here's what's okay: If we feel there's corruption, like I feel there was in the 2016 campaign—there was tremendous corruption against me—if we feel there's corruption, we have a right to go to a foreign country."[230]

144.   As the House's impeachment inquiry unfolded, Mr. Giuliani, on behalf of the President, also continued to urge Ukraine to pursue the investigations and dig up dirt on former

---

[227] *Remarks by President Trump Before Marine One Departure*, White House (Oct. 3, 2019) (Trump Oct. 3 Remarks), https://perma.cc/WM8A-NRA2.

[228] *Id.*

[229] *Remarks by President Trump Before Marine One Departure*, White House (Oct. 4, 2019) (Trump Oct. 4 Remarks), https://perma.cc/C78K-NMDS.

[230] *Id.*

Vice President Biden. Mr. Giuliani's own statements about these efforts further confirm that he has been working in furtherance of the President's personal and political interests.[231]

145.   During the first week of December, Mr. Giuliani traveled to Kyiv and Budapest to meet with both current and former Ukrainian government officials,[232] including a current Ukrainian member of Parliament who attended a KGB school in Moscow and has led calls to investigate Burisma and the Bidens.[233] Mr. Giuliani also met with the corrupt former prosecutor generals, Viktor Shokin and Yuriy Lutsenko, who had promoted the false allegations underlying the investigations President Trump wanted.[234] Mr. Giuliani told the *New York Times* that in meeting with Ukrainian officials he was acting on behalf of his client, President Trump: "[L]ike a good lawyer, I am gathering evidence to defend my client against the false charges being leveled against him."[235]

146.   During his trip to Ukraine, on December 5, Mr. Giuliani tweeted: "The conversation about corruption in Ukraine was based on compelling evidence of criminal conduct by then VP Biden, in 2016, that has not been resolved and until it is will be a major obstacle to the US assisting Ukraine with its anti-corruption reforms."[236] Not only was Mr. Giuliani perpetuating the

---

[231] *See, e.g.*, Kenneth P. Vogel & Benjamin Novak, *Giuliani, Facing Scrutiny, Travels to Europe to Interview Ukrainians*, N.Y. Times (Dec. 4, 2019) (*Giuliani, Facing Scrutiny, Travels to Europe*), https://perma.cc/N28V-GPAC; Dana Bash & Michael Warren, *Giuliani Says Trump Still Supports His Dirt-Digging in Ukraine*, CNN (Dec. 17, 2019) (*Giuliani Says Trump Still Supports His Dirt-Digging*), https://perma.cc/F399-B9AY.

[232] *Giuliani, Facing Scrutiny, Travels to Europe*, https://perma.cc/HZ6F-E67G; David L. Stern & Robyn Dixon, *Ukraine Lawmaker Seeking Biden Probe Meets with Giuliani in Kyiv*, Wash. Post (Dec. 5, 2019) (*Ukraine Lawmaker Seeking Biden Probe*), https://perma.cc/C3GW-RF4T; Will Sommer, *Rudy's New Ukraine Jaunt Is Freaking Out Trump's Lieutenants—and He Doesn't Care*, Daily Beast (Dec. 6, 2019) (*Rudy's New Ukraine Jaunt*), https://perma.cc/UNR9-VWFZ.

[233] *Ukraine Lawmaker Seeking Biden Probe*, https://perma.cc/W3Q2-E8QY.

[234] Philip Bump, *Giuliani May Be Making a Stronger Case Against Trump Than Biden*, Wash. Post (Dec. 16, 2019), https://perma.cc/7HR4-TC9W; *Rudy's New Ukraine Jaunt*, https://perma.cc/UNR9-VWFZ.

[235] *Giuliani, Facing Scrutiny, Travels to Europe*, https://perma.cc/HZ6F-E67G.

[236] Rudy Giuliani (@RudyGiuliani), Twitter (Dec. 5, 2019, 1:42 PM), https://perma.cc/829X-TSKJ.

false allegations against Vice President Biden, but he was reiterating the threat that President Trump had used to pressure President Zelensky to announce the investigations: that U.S. assistance to Ukraine could be in jeopardy until Ukraine investigated Vice President Biden.

147. Mr. Giuliani told the *Wall Street Journal* that when he returned to New York on December 7, President Trump called him as his plane was still taxiing down the runway. "'What did you get?' he said Mr. Trump asked. 'More than you can imagine,' Mr. Giuliani replied."[237]

148. Later that day, President Trump told reporters that he was aware of Mr. Giuliani's efforts in Ukraine and believed that Mr. Giuliani wanted to report the information he'd gathered to the Attorney General and Congress.[238]

149. On December 17, Mr. Giuliani confirmed that President Trump has been "very supportive" of his continuing efforts to dig up dirt on Vice President Biden in Ukraine and that they are "on the same page."[239]

150. Such ongoing efforts by President Trump, including through his personal attorney, to solicit an investigation of his political opponent have undermined U.S. credibility. On September 14, Ambassador Volker advised Mr. Yermak against the Zelensky Administration conducting an investigation into President Zelensky's own former political rival, former Ukrainian President Petro Poroshenko. When Ambassador Volker raised concerns about such an investigation, Mr. Yermak

---

[237] Rebecca Ballhaus & Julie Bykowicz, *"Just Having Fun": Giuliani Doubles Down on Ukraine Probes*, Wall Street J. (Dec. 13, 2019), https://perma.cc/5B69-2AVR.

[238] David Jackson, *Trump Says Rudy Giuliani Will Give Information About Ukraine to Justice Department, Congress*, USA Today (Dec. 7, 2019), https://perma.cc/7RXJ-JG7F.

[239] *Giuliani Says Trump Still Supports His Dirt-Digging*, https://perma.cc/F399-B9AY; *see also* Asawin Suebsaeng & Erin Banco, *Trump Tells Rudy to Keep Pushing the Biden Conspiracies*, Daily Beast (Dec. 18, 2019), https://perma.cc/S5K6-K8J9 (quoting source who reported that President Trump told Mr. Giuliani to "keep at it").

retorted, "What, you mean like asking us to investigate Clinton and Biden?"[240] Ambassador Volker

offered no response.[241]

151.   Mr. Holmes, a career diplomat, highlighted this hypocrisy: "While we had advised

our Ukrainian counterparts to voice a commitment to following the rule of law and generally

investigating credible corruption allegations," U.S. officials were making "a demand that President

Zelensky personally commit on a cable news channel to a specific investigation of President

Trump's political rival."[242]

H.   President Trump's Conduct Was Consistent with His Previous Invitations of Foreign Interference in U.S. Elections

152.   President Trump's efforts to solicit Ukraine's interference in the 2020 U.S.

Presidential election to help his own reelection campaign were consistent with his prior solicitation

and encouragement of Russia's interference in the 2016 election, when the Trump Campaign

"expected it would benefit electorally from information stolen and released through Russian

efforts."[243]

153.   As a Presidential candidate, Mr. Trump repeatedly sought to benefit from Russia's

actions to help his campaign. For example, during a public rally on July 27, 2016, then-candidate

Trump declared: "Russia, if you're listening, I hope you're able to find the 30,000 emails that are

missing" from opposing candidate Hillary Clinton's personal server.[244] Within hours, Russian

hackers targeted Clinton's personal office for the first time.[245]

---

[240] Volker-Morrison Hearing Tr. at 139; *see* Kent Dep. Tr. at 329.
[241] Kent Dep. Tr. at 329.
[242] Hill-Holmes Hearing Tr. at 32.
[243] Mueller Report, Vol. I at 1-2.
[244] Mueller Report, Vol. I at 49 (quoting then-candidate Donald Trump).
[245] *Id.* Beginning in early November 2019, while the House's impeachment inquiry was ongoing, Russian military hackers reportedly hacked Burisma's server using "strikingly similar" tactics to those used to hack the DNC in 2016. *See* Nicole Perlroth & Matthew Rosenberg, *Russians*

154. Days earlier, WikiLeaks had begun releasing emails and documents that were stolen by Russian military intelligence services in order to damage the Clinton campaign.[246] WikiLeaks continued releasing stolen documents through October 2016.[247] Then-candidate Trump repeatedly applauded and sought to capitalize on WikiLeaks's releases of these stolen documents, even after Russia's involvement was heavily reported by the press.[248] Members of the Trump Campaign also planned messaging and communications strategies around releases by WikiLeaks.[249] In the last month of the campaign, then-candidate Trump publicly referred to the emails hacked by Russia and disseminated by WikiLeaks over 150 times.[250]

155. Multiple members of the Trump Campaign used additional channels to seek Russia's assistance in obtaining damaging information about Clinton. For example, senior representatives of the Trump Campaign—including the Campaign's chairman and the President's son—met with a Russian attorney in June 2016 who had offered to provide damaging information about Clinton from the Russian government.[251] A foreign policy advisor to the Trump Campaign also met repeatedly with people connected to the Russian government and their associates, one of whom claimed to have "dirt" on Clinton in the form of "thousands of emails."[252]

156. Even after Special Counsel Mueller released his report, President Trump confirmed his willingness to benefit from foreign election interference. When asked during a televised

Hacked Ukrainian Gas Company at Center of Impeachment, N.Y. Times (Jan. 13, 2019), https://perma.cc/5NSA-BELW.

[246] Mueller Report, Vol. I at 6.

[247] *Id.*, Vol. I at 58.

[248] *See* Aaron Blake, *The Trump Team's History of Flirting with—and Promoting—Now-Accused-Criminal Julian Assange*, Wash. Post (Nov. 16, 2018), https://perma.cc/UL9R-YQN.

[249] Mueller Report, Vol. I at 54; *id.*, Vol. II at 18.

[250] Judd Legum, *Trump Mentioned WikiLeaks 164 Times in Last Month of Election, Now Claims It Didn't Impact One Voter*, ThinkProgress (Jan. 8, 2017), https://perma.cc/5J46-Y8RG.

[251] Mueller Report, Vol. I at 110-20.

[252] *Id.*, Vol. I at 83-84, 87-89.

interview in June 2019 whether he would accept damaging information from a foreign government about a political opponent, the President responded, "I think I'd take it."[253] President Trump declared that he sees "nothing wrong with listening" to a foreign power that offers information detrimental to a political adversary.[254] Asked whether such an offer of information should be reported to law enforcement, President Trump retorted: "Give me a break, life doesn't work that way."[255] Just weeks later, President Trump froze security assistance to Ukraine as his agents were pushing that country to pursue investigations that would help the President's reelection campaign.[256]

157.   In addition, President Trump's request for the investigations on the July 25 call with President Zelensky took place one day after former Special Counsel Mueller testified before the House Judiciary Committee and the House Permanent Select Committee on Intelligence about the findings of his investigation into Russia's interference in the 2016 Presidential election and President Trump's efforts to undermine that investigation.[257] During his call with President Zelensky, President Trump derided former Special Counsel Mueller's "poor performance" in his July 24 testimony and speculated that "that whole nonsense . . . started with Ukraine."[258]

II.   PRESIDENT TRUMP'S OBSTRUCTION OF CONGRESS

158.   President Trump ordered categorical obstruction of the impeachment inquiry undertaken by the House under Article I of the Constitution, which vests the House with the "sole Power of Impeachment."[259]

---

[253] *Transcript: ABC News' George Stephanopoulos' Exclusive Interview with President Trump*, ABC News (June 16, 2019), https://perma.cc/C8DS-637R.

[254] *Id.*

[255] *Id.*

[256] Sandy Dep. Tr. at 37-39; Morrison Dep. Tr. at 161.

[257] *See* Press Release, House Permanent Select Comm. on Intelligence, House Judiciary and House Intelligence Committees to Hold Open Hearing with Special Counsel Robert Mueller (July 19, 2019), https://perma.cc/6TZZ-BJKS.

[258] The July 25 Memorandum at 3, https://perma.cc/8JRD-6K9V.

[259] U.S. Const., Art. I, § 2, cl. 5.

A. The House Launched an Impeachment Inquiry

159. During the 116th Congress, a number of Committees of the House have undertaken investigations into allegations of misconduct by President Trump and his Administration, including to determine whether to recommend articles of impeachment.[260]

160. As discussed above, on September 9, the Intelligence Committee and the Committees on Oversight and Reform and Foreign Affairs announced they would conduct a joint investigation into the President's scheme to pressure Ukraine to announce the politically motivated investigations.[261]

161. Given the gravity of the allegations that President Trump was soliciting foreign interference in the upcoming 2020 election, Speaker Nancy P. Pelosi announced on September 24 that the House was "moving forward with an official impeachment inquiry."[262] Speaker Pelosi directed the Committees to "proceed with their investigations under that umbrella of [an] impeachment inquiry."[263]

162. On October 31, the House enacted a resolution confirming the Committees' authority to conduct the impeachment inquiry and adopting procedures governing the inquiry.[264]

---

[260] *See, e.g., Resolution Recommending That the House of Representatives Find William P. Barr, Attorney General, U.S. Department of Justice, in Contempt of Congress for Refusal to Comply with a Subpoena Duly Issued by the Committee on the Judiciary*, H. Rep. No. 116-105, at 13 (June 6, 2019) ("The purposes of this investigation include . . . considering whether any of the conduct described in the Special Counsel's Report warrants the Committee in taking any further steps under Congress' Article I powers. That includes whether to approve articles of impeachment with respect to the President[.]"); *Directing Certain Committees to Continue Their Ongoing Investigations as Part of the Existing House of Representatives Inquiry into Whether Sufficient Grounds Exist for the House of Representatives to Exercise its Constitutional Power to Impeach Donald John Trump, President of the United States of America, and for Other Purposes*, H. Rep. No. 116-266, at 4 (Oct. 2019).

[261] Sept. 9 Press Release, https://perma.cc/AX4Y-PWSH.

[262] Press Release, Speaker of the House, Pelosi Remarks Announcing Impeachment Inquiry (Sept. 24, 2019), https://perma.cc/6EQM-34PT.

[263] *Id.*

[264] H. Res. 660, 116th Cong. (2019).

163. The procedures adopted by the House afforded procedural privileges to the President that were equivalent to, or in some instances exceeded, those afforded during prior impeachment inquiries.[265] Transcripts of all witness interviews and depositions were released to the public, and President Trump was offered—but refused—multiple opportunities to have his counsel participate in proceedings before the Judiciary Committee, including by cross-examining witnesses and presenting evidence.[266]

B. President Trump Ordered Categorical Obstruction of the House's Impeachment Inquiry

164. Even before the House launched its impeachment inquiry into President Trump's misconduct concerning Ukraine, he rejected Congress's Article I investigative and oversight authority, proclaiming, "[W]e're fighting all the subpoenas,"[267] and "I have an Article II, where I have the right to do whatever I want as president."[268]

165. In response to the House impeachment inquiry regarding Ukraine, the Executive Branch categorically refused to provide any requested documents or information at President Trump's direction.

166. On September 9, 2019, three House Committees sent a letter to White House Counsel Pat Cipollone requesting six categories of documents relevant to the Ukraine investigation

---

[265] *Compare* 165 Cong. Rec. E1357 (2019) (Impeachment Inquiry Procedures in the Committee on the Judiciary Pursuant to H. Res. 660), *with Investigatory Powers of the Committee on the Judiciary with Respect to Its Impeachment Inquiry*, H. Rep. No. 105-795 (1998), *and with Impeachment Inquiry: Hearings Before the H. Comm. on the Judiciary, Book III*, 93d Cong. 2249-52 (1974); *see also* H. Rep. No. 116-346, at 17-25.

[266] H. Rep. No. 116-346, at 22-24.

[267] *Remarks by President Trump Before Marine One Departure*, White House (Apr. 24, 2019), https://perma.cc/W7VZ-FZ3T.

[268] *Remarks by President Trump at Turning Point USA's Teen Student Action Summit 2019*, White House (July 23, 2019), https://perma.cc/EFF6-9BE7.

by September 16.[269] When the White House did not respond, the Committees sent a follow-up

letter on September 24.[270]

167.   Instead of responding directly to the Committees, the President publicly declared the

impeachment inquiry "a disgrace," and stated that "it shouldn't be allowed" and that "[t]here should

be a way of stopping it."[271]

168.   When the White House still did not respond to the Committees' request, the

Committees issued a subpoena compelling the White House to turn over documents.[272]

169.   The President's response to the House's inquiry—sent by Mr. Cipollone on October

8—sought to accomplish the President's goal of "stopping" the House's investigation. Mr.

Cipollone wrote "on behalf of President Donald J. Trump" to notify Congress that "President

Trump cannot permit his Administration to participate in this partisan inquiry under these

circumstances."[273]

170.   Despite the Constitution's placement of the "sole Power" of impeachment in the

House, Mr. Cipollone's October 8 letter opined that the House's inquiry was "constitutionally

invalid," "lack[ed] . . . any basis," "lack[ed] the necessary authorization for a valid impeachment,"

and was merely "labeled . . . as an 'impeachment inquiry.'"[274]

---

[269] Sept. 9 Letter, https://perma.cc/R2GH-TZ9P.

[270] Letter from Chairman Eliot L. Engel, House Comm. on Foreign Affairs, et al., to Pat A.
Cipollone, Counsel to the President 3 (Sept. 24, 2019), https://perma.cc/SCG3-6UEW.

[271] *Remarks by President Trump upon Air Force One Arrival*, White House (Sept. 26, 2019),
https://perma.cc/5RWE-8VTB.

[272] Letter from Chairman Elijah E. Cummings, House Comm. on Oversight and Reform, et
al., to John Michael Mulvaney, Acting Chief of Staff to the President (Oct. 4, 2019) (Oct. 4 Letter),
https://perma.cc/6RXE-WER8.

[273] Letter from Pat A. Cipollone, Counsel to the President, to Speaker Nancy Pelosi, House
of Representatives, et al. 7 (Oct. 8, 2019), https://perma.cc/5P57-773X (Oct. 8 Cipollone Letter).

[274] *Id.* at 1-3, 6.

171. The letter's rhetoric aligned with the President's public campaign against the impeachment inquiry, which he has branded "a COUP, intended to take away the Power of the People,"[275] an "unconstitutional abuse of power,"[276] and an "open war on American Democracy."[277]

172. Although President Trump has categorically sought to obstruct the House's impeachment inquiry, he has never formally asserted a claim of executive privilege as to any document or testimony. Mr. Cipollone's October 8 letter refers to "long-established Executive Branch confidentiality interests and privileges" but the President did not actually assert executive privilege.[278] Similarly, a Department of Justice Office of Legal Counsel November 1, 2019 opinion only recognized that information responsive to the subpoenas was "*potentially* protected by executive privilege."[279]

173. In addition, the President and his agents have spoken at length about these events to the press and on social media. Since the impeachment inquiry was announced on September 24, the President has made numerous public statements about his communications with President Zelensky and his decision-making relating to the hold on security assistance.[280]

174. The President's agents have done the same. For example, on October 16, Secretary Perry gave an interview to the *Wall Street Journal*. During the interview, Secretary Perry stated that

---

[275] @realDonaldTrump (Oct. 1, 2019, 4:41 PM), https://perma.cc/UX8Z-BFKL.

[276] Letter from President Donald J. Trump to Speaker Nancy Pelosi, House of Representatives (Dec. 17, 2019), https://perma.cc/MY49-HRXH.

[277] *Id.*

[278] Oct. 8 Cipollone Letter at 4.

[279] Exclusion of Agency Counsel from Congressional Depositions in the Impeachment Context, 43 O.L.C. *1 (Nov. 1, 2019), https://perma.cc/T2PH-KC9V (emphasis added).

[280] *See, e.g.*, Trump Sept. 25 Remarks, https://perma.cc/XCJ4-A67L; Trump Sept. 30 Remarks, https://perma.cc/R94C-5HAY; *Remarks by President Trump and President Niinistö of the Republic of Finland Before Bilateral Meeting*, White House (Oct. 2, 2019), https://perma.cc/FN4D-6D8W; Trump Oct. 3 Remarks, https://perma.cc/WM8A-NRA2; Trump Oct. 4 Remarks, https://perma.cc/C78K-NMDS; @realDonaldTrump (Nov. 10, 2019, 11:43 AM), https://perma.cc/F9XH-48Z2; *id.* (Dec. 4, 2019, 7:50 PM), https://perma.cc/Q4VY-T3CN; *id.*, https://perma.cc/3WCM-AQJG.

after the May 23 meeting at which President Trump refused to schedule a White House meeting with President Zelensky, Secretary Perry "sought out Rudy Giuliani this spring at President Trump's direction to address Mr. Trump's concerns about alleged Ukrainian corruption."[281] During a phone call with Secretary Perry, Mr. Giuliani said, "'Look, the president is really concerned that there are people in Ukraine that tried to beat him during this presidential election. . . . He thinks they're corrupt and . . . that there are still people over there engaged that are absolutely corrupt.'"[282]

175.   On October 17, Acting Chief of Staff Mulvaney acknowledged during a White House press conference that he discussed security assistance with the President and that the President's decision to withhold it was directly tied to his desire that Ukraine investigate alleged Ukrainian interference in the 2016 U.S. election.[283]

176.   On December 3, 2019, the Intelligence Committee transmitted a detailed nearly 300-page report documenting its findings about this scheme and about the related investigation into it, to the Judiciary Committee.[284] The Judiciary Committee held public hearings evaluating the constitutional standard for impeachment and the evidence against President Trump—in which the President's counsel was invited to participate, but declined—and then reported two Articles of Impeachment to the House.[285]

---

[281] *Rick Perry Called Rudy Giuliani*, https://perma.cc/S2ED-AUPR.
[282] *Id.* (quoting Secretary Rick Perry).
[283] Oct. 17 Briefing, https://perma.cc/Q45H-EMC7.
[284] H. Rep. No. 116-346, at 11 ("On December 3, 2019, in consultation with the Committees on Oversight and Reform and Foreign Affairs, HPSCI released and voted to adopt a report of nearly 300 pages detailing its extensive findings about the President's abuse of his office and obstruction of Congress.").
[285] *The Impeachment Inquiry into President Donald J. Trump: Constitutional Grounds for Presidential Impeachment: Hearing Before the H. Comm. on the Judiciary*, 116th Cong. (Dec. 4, 2019); *The Impeachment Inquiry into President Donald J. Trump: Presentations from H. Permanent Select Comm. on Intelligence and H. Comm. on the Judiciary Before the H. Comm. on the Judiciary*, 116th Cong. (Dec. 9, 2019).

177.   The President maintained his obstructionist position throughout this process, declaring the House's investigation "illegitimate" in a letter to Speaker Nancy Pelosi on December 17, 2019.[286] President Trump further attempted to undermine the House's inquiry by dismissing impeachment as "illegal, invalid, and unconstitutional"[287] and by intimidating and threatening an anonymous Intelligence Community whistleblower as well as the patriotic public servants who honored their subpoenas and testified before the House.[288]

178.   On December 18, 2019, the House voted to impeach President Trump and adopted two Articles of Impeachment.[289]

C.   Following President Trump's Directive, the Executive Branch Refused to Produce Requested and Subpoenaed Documents

179.   Adhering to President Trump's directive, every Executive Branch agency that received an impeachment inquiry request or subpoena defied it.[290]

180.   House Committees issued document requests or subpoenas to the White House, the Office of the Vice President, OMB, the Department of State, DOD, and the Department of Energy.[291]

---

[286] *See, e.g.*, Letter from President Donald J. Trump to Speaker Nancy Pelosi, U.S. House of Representatives (Dec. 17, 2019), https://perma.cc/Y6X4-TTPR.

[287] Katie Rogers, *At Louisiana Rally, Trump Lashes Out at Impeachment Inquiry and Pelosi*, N.Y. TIMES (Oct. 11, 2019), https://perma.cc/RX9Z-DQHK.

[288] *See e.g.*, Danny Cevallos, *Trump Tweeted as Marie Yovanovitch Testified: Was It Witness Tampering?*, NBC News (Nov. 16, 2019), https://perma.cc/RG5N-EQYN; @realDonaldTrump (Sept. 29, 2019, 3:53 PM), https://perma.cc/9C3P-E437; Trump War Room—Text FIGHT to 88022 (@TrumpWarRoom) (Dec. 26, 2019, 1:50 PM), https://perma.cc/M5H7-B4VS (retweeted by @realDonaldTrump on Dec. 26, 2019).

[289] H. Res. 755, 116th Cong (2019).

[290] *See* H. Rep. No. 116-335, at 180-92.

[291] Oct. 4 Letter, https://perma.cc/6RXE-WER8; Letter from Chairman Eliot L. Engel, House Comm. on Foreign Affairs, et al., to Vice President Michael R. Pence (Oct. 4, 2019), https://perma.cc/E6TR-5N5F; Letter from Chairman Adam B. Schiff, House Permanent Select Comm. on Intelligence, et al., to Russell T. Vought, Acting Dir., Office of Mgmt. & Budget (Oct. 7, 2019), https://perma.cc/2HBV-2LNB; Letter from Chairman Eliot L. Engel, House Comm. on Foreign Affairs, et al., to Michael R. Pompeo, Sec'y, Dep't of State (Sept. 27, 2019),

181.   In its response, the Office of the Vice President echoed Mr. Cipollone's assertions

that the impeachment inquiry was procedurally invalid,[292] while agencies such as OMB and DOD

expressly cited the President's directive.[293]

182.   The Executive Branch has refused to produce any documents in response to the

Committees' valid, legally binding subpoenas, even though witness testimony has revealed that

highly relevant records exist.[294]

183.   Indeed, by virtue of President Trump's order, not a single document has been

produced by the White House, the Office of the Vice President, OMB, the Department of State,

---

https://perma.cc/8N7L-VSDR; Letter from Chairman Adam B. Schiff, House Permanent Select
Comm. on Intelligence, et al., to Mark Esper, Sec'y, Dep't of Def. (Oct. 7, 2019),
https://perma.cc/LMU8-XWE9; Letter from Chairman Eliot L. Engel, House Comm. on Foreign
Affairs, et al., to Rick Perry, Sec'y, Dep't of Energy (Oct. 10, 2019), https://perma.cc/586S-AR8A.

[292] Letter from Matthew E. Morgan, Counsel to the Vice President, to Chairman Elijah E.
Cummings, House Comm. on Oversight and Reform, et al. (Oct. 15, 2019),
https://perma.cc/L6LD-C4YM.

[293] Letter from Jason Yaworske, Assoc. Dir. for Legislative Affairs, Office of Mgmt. &
Budget, to Chairman Adam B. Schiff, House Permanent Select Comm. on Intelligence (Oct. 15,
2019), https://perma.cc/AL7W-YBLR; Letter from Robert R. Hood, Assistant Sec'y of Def. for
Legislative Affairs, Dep't of Def., to Chairman Adam B. Schiff, House Permanent Select Comm. on
Intelligence, et al. (Oct. 15, 2019), https://perma.cc/79ZG-ASGM.

[294] *See, e.g.*, Vindman-Williams Hearing Tr. at 31-32 (briefing materials for President Trump's
call with President Zelensky on July 25 prepared by Lt. Col. Vindman, Director for Ukraine at the
NSC); Vindman Dep. Tr. at 53 and Morrison Dep. Tr. at 19-20 (notes relating to the July 25 call
taken by Lt. Col. Vindman and Mr. Morrison, the former Senior Director for Europe and Russia on
the NSC); Vindman Dep. Tr. at 186-87 and Morrison Dep. Tr. at 166-67 (an August 15 "Presidential
decision memo" prepared by Lt. Col. Vindman and approved by Mr. Morrison conveying "the
consensus views from the entire deputies small group" that "the security assistance be released");
Cooper Dep. Tr. at 42-43 (NSC staff summaries of conclusions from meetings at the principal,
deputy, or sub-deputy level relating to Ukraine, including military assistance); Sondland Hearing Tr.
at 78-79 (call records between President Trump and Ambassador Sondland,); Vindman Dep. Tr. at
36-37 (NSC Legal Advisor Eisenberg's notes and correspondence relating to discussions with Lt.
Col. Vindman regarding the July 10 meetings in which Ambassador Sondland requested
investigations in exchange for a White House meeting); Holmes Dep. Tr. at 31 (the memorandum of
conversation from President Trump's meeting in New York with President Zelensky on September
25); Sondland Opening Statement (emails and other messages between Ambassador Sondland and
senior White House officials, including Acting Chief of Staff Mulvaney, Senior Advisor to the Chief
of Staff Blair, and then-National Security Advisor Bolton, among other high-level Trump
Administration officials).

DOD, or the Department of Energy in response to 71 specific, individualized requests or demands for records in their possession, custody, or control. These agencies and offices also blocked many current and former officials from producing records to the Committees.[295]

184. Certain witnesses, however, defied the President's order and identified the substance of key documents. For example, Lt. Col. Vindman described a "Presidential Decision Memo" he prepared in August that conveyed the "consensus views" among foreign policy and national security officials that the hold on aid to Ukraine should be released.[296] Other witnesses identified additional documents that the President and various agencies were withholding from Congress that were directly relevant to the impeachment inquiry.[297]

185. Some responsive documents have been released by the State Department, DOD, and OMB pursuant to judicial orders issued in response to lawsuits filed under the Freedom of Information Act (FOIA).[298] Although limited in scope and heavily redacted, these FOIA productions confirm that the Trump Administration is withholding highly pertinent documents from Congress without any valid legal basis.[299]

---

[295] *See* H. Rep. No. 116-335, at 180-244.

[296] Vindman Dep. Tr. at 186-87; Morrison Dep. Tr. at 166-67; *see also, e.g.,* Sandy Dep. Tr. at 58-60 (describing an OMB memorandum prepared in August that recommended removing the hold).

[297] Taylor Dep. Tr. at 33-34, 45-46 (describing August 27 cable to Secretary Pompeo, WhatsApp messages with Ukrainian and American officials, and notes); Volker Dep. Tr. at 20 (describing State Department's possession of substantial paper trail of correspondence concerning meetings with Ukraine); Yovanovitch Dep. Tr. at 61 (describing classified email to Under Secretary Hale); *id.* at 197-200 (describing a dispute between George Kent and the State Department pertaining to subpoenaed documents).

[298] *See, e.g., State Department Releases Ukraine Documents to American Oversight*, American Oversight (Nov. 22, 2019), https://perma.cc/N7K2-D7G3; Joint Status Report at 1, American Oversight v. Dep't of State, No. 19-cv-2934 (D.D.C. Nov. 25, 2019), ECF No. 19.

[299] For example, documents produced by OMB, unredacted copies of which reportedly were obtained by the online forum *Just Security*, corroborate the witnesses who testified that the military aid for Ukraine was withheld at the express direction of President Trump and that the White House was informed that doing so may violate the law. *See* Just Security Report, https://perma.cc/VA6U-RYPK.

D. President Trump Ordered Top Aides Not to Testify, Even Pursuant to Subpoena

186. President Trump directed government witnesses to violate their legal obligations and defy House subpoenas—regardless of their offices or positions. In some instances, the President personally directed that senior aides defy subpoenas on the ground that they are "absolutely immune" from compelled testimony.[300] Other officials refused to appear "as directed by" Mr. Cipollone's October 8 letter.[301] Still others refused to appear because—consistent with the House Deposition Rules drafted by the then-majority Republicans—agency counsel was not permitted in the depositions.[302]

187. This Administration-wide effort to prevent witnesses from providing testimony was coordinated and comprehensive. In total, twelve current or former Administration officials refused to testify as part of the House's impeachment inquiry into the Ukrainian matter, nine of whom did so in defiance of duly authorized subpoenas.[303] House Committees advised such witnesses that their refusal to testify may be used as an adverse inference against the President.[304] Nonetheless—despite

---

[300] *See* Letter from Pat A. Cipollone, Counsel to the President, to William Pittard, Counsel to Acting Chief of Staff Mick Mulvaney (Nov. 8, 2019), https://perma.cc/9PHC-84AM; Letter from Pat A. Cipollone, Counsel to the President, to William Burck, Counsel to Deputy Counsel to the President for Nat'l Security Affairs John Eisenberg (Nov. 3, 2019), https://perma.cc/QP4G-YMKQ.

[301] *See, e.g.*, Letter from Jason A. Yaworske, Associate Dir. for Leg. Affairs, Office of Mgmt. & Budget, to Chairman Adam B. Schiff, House Permanent Select Comm. on Intelligence (Nov. 4, 2019), https://perma.cc/4AYC-8SD9 (asserting OMB's "position that, as directed by the White House Counsel's October 8, 2019 letter, OMB will not participate in this partisan and unfair inquiry," and that three OMB officials would therefore defy subpoenas for their testimony).

[302] *See* H. Rep. No. 116-335, at 195, 198-99, 201, 203. Such witnesses included Robert Blair, Michael Ellis, P. Wells Griffith, Russell Vought, and Brian McCormack. *Id.*

[303] *See id.* at 193-206 (describing and quoting from correspondence with each witness who refused to appear).

[304] *See* H. Rep. No. 116-346, at 200, 365; *see, e.g.*, Letter from Chairman Adam B. Schiff, House Permanent Select Comm. on Intelligence, et al., to Michael Duffey, Assoc. Dir. for Nat'l Sec. Programs, Office of Mgmt. & Budget (Oct. 25, 2019), https://perma.cc/3S5B-FH94; Email from Daniel S. Noble, Senior Investigative Counsel, House Permanent Select Comm. on Intelligence, to

being instructed by senior political appointees not to cooperate with the House's impeachment inquiry, in directives that frequently cited or enclosed copies of Mr. Cipollone's October 8 letter[305]— many current and former officials complied with their legal obligations to appear for testimony.

188.   House Committees conducted depositions or transcribed interviews of seventeen witnesses.[306] All members of the Committees—as well as staff from the Majority and the Minority—were permitted to attend. The Majority and Minority were allotted an equal amount of time to question witnesses.[307]

189.   In late November 2019, twelve of these witnesses testified in public hearings convened by the Intelligence Committee, including three witnesses called by the Minority.[308]

190.   Unable to silence certain witnesses, President Trump resorted to intimidation tactics to penalize them.[309] He also levied sustained attacks on the anonymous whistleblower.[310]

Mick Mulvaney, Acting Chief of Staff to the President (Nov. 7, 2019), https://perma.cc/A62P-5ACG.

[305] *See, e.g.*, Letter from Brian Bulatao, Under Sec'y of State for Mgmt., Dep't of State, to Lawrence S. Robbins, Counsel to Ambassador Marie Yovanovitch 1 (Oct. 10, 2019), https://perma.cc/48UC-KJCM ("I write on behalf of the Department of State, pursuant to the President's instruction reflected in Mr. Cipollone's letter, to instruct your client . . . consistent with Mr. Cipollone's letter, not to appear before the Committees."); *id.* at 3-10 (enclosing Mr. Cipollone's letter); Letter from David L. Norquist, Deputy Sec'y of Def., Dep't of Def., to Daniel Levin, Counsel to Deputy Assistant Sec'y of Def. Laura K. Cooper 1-2 (Oct. 22, 2019), https://perma.cc/WM97-DZJZ ("This letter informs you and Ms. Cooper of the Administration-wide direction that Executive Branch personnel 'cannot participate in [the impeachment] inquiry under these circumstances.'" (quoting Mr. Cipollone's letter)); *id.* at 25-32 (enclosing Mr. Cipollone's letter).

[306] *See* H. Rep. No. 116-346, at 9; *see also Read for Yourself: President Trump's Abuse of Power*, House Permanent Select Comm. on Intelligence, https://perma.cc/2L54-YY9P.

[307] *See* H. Rep. No. 116-346, at 9.

[308] *See id.* at 10-11.

[309] *See* H. Rep. No. 116-335, at 217-20 (detailing the ways that "President Trump publicly attacked and intimidated witnesses who came forward to comply with duly authorized subpoenas and testify about his conduct."); H. Rep. No. 116-346, at 366-67.

[310] *See* H. Rep. No. 116-335, at 221-23 (detailing the ways that President Trump "threatened and attacked an Intelligence Community whistleblower"); H. Rep. No. 116-346, at 366-67.

E.   President Trump's Conduct Was Consistent with His Previous Efforts to Obstruct Investigations into Foreign Interference in U.S. Elections

191.   President Trump's obstruction of the House's impeachment inquiry was consistent with his previous efforts to undermine Special Counsel Mueller's investigation of Russia's interference in the 2016 election and of the President's own misconduct.

192.   President Trump repeatedly used his powers of office to undermine and derail the Mueller investigation, particularly after learning that he was personally under investigation for obstruction of justice.[311] Among other things, President Trump ordered White House Counsel Don McGahn to fire Special Counsel Mueller;[312] instructed Mr. McGahn to create a record and issue statements falsely denying this event;[313] sought to curtail Special Counsel Mueller's investigation in a manner exempting his own prior conduct;[314] and tampered with at least two key witnesses.[315] President Trump has since instructed McGahn to defy a House Committee's subpoena for testimony, and his DOJ has erroneously argued that the courts can play no role in enforcing Congressional subpoenas.[316]

193.   Special Counsel Mueller's investigation—like the House's impeachment inquiry—sought to uncover whether President Trump coordinated with a foreign government in order to obtain an improper advantage during a Presidential election.[317] And the Mueller investigation—like the House's impeachment inquiry—exposed President Trump's eagerness to benefit from foreign

---

[311] *See generally* Mueller Report, Vol. II; H. Rep. No. 116-346, at 159-61.

[312] Mueller Report, Vol. II at 85-86.

[313] *Id.*, Vol. II at 114-17.

[314] *Id.*, Vol. II at 90-93.

[315] *Id.*, Vol. II at 120-56.

[316] *See* Comm. on the Judiciary v. McGahn, — F. Supp. 3d —, No. 19-2379. 2019 WL 6312011 (D.D.C. Nov. 25, 2019), *appeal pending*, No. 19-5331 (D.C. Cir.). The U.S. Court of Appeals for the D.C. Circuit heard oral argument in the case on January 3, 2020.

[317] Mueller Report, Vol. I at 1 (describing the scope of the order appointing Special Counsel Mueller).

election interference.[318] In the former instance, the President used his powers of office to undermine an investigation conducted by officials within the Executive Branch.[319] In the latter, he attempted to block the United States House of Representatives from exercising its "sole Power of Impeachment" assigned by the Constitution. In both instances, President Trump obstructed investigations into foreign election interference to hide his own misconduct.

---

[318] *See, e.g., id.*, Vol. I at 1-2 (the Trump Campaign "expected it would benefit electorally from information stolen and released through Russian efforts").

[319] *See generally id.*, Vol. II. As the Mueller Report summarizes, the Special Counsel's investigation "found multiple acts by the President that were capable of exerting undue influence over law enforcement investigations, including the Russian-interference and obstruction investigations. The incidents were often carried out through one-on-one meetings in which the President sought to use his official power outside of usual channels. These actions ranged from efforts to remove the Special Counsel and to reverse the effect of the Attorney General's recusal; to the attempted use of official power to limit the scope of the investigation; to direct and indirect contacts with witnesses with the potential to influence their testimony." *Id.*, Vol. II at 157.

IN THE SENATE OF THE UNITED STATES
Sitting as a Court of Impeachment

In re

**IMPEACHMENT OF
PRESIDENT DONALD J. TRUMP**

REPLY MEMORANDUM OF THE
UNITED STATES HOUSE OF REPRESENTATIVES
IN THE IMPEACHMENT TRIAL OF PRESIDENT DONALD J. TRUMP

United States House of Representatives

Adam B. Schiff
Jerrold Nadler
Zoe Lofgren
Hakeem S. Jeffries
Val Butler Demings
Jason Crow
Sylvia R. Garcia

U.S. House of Representatives Managers

TABLE OF CONTENTS

INTRODUCTION 1

ARGUMENT 6

I.   PRESIDENT TRUMP MUST BE REMOVED FOR ABUSING HIS POWER 6

    A.   President Trump's Abuse of Power Is a Quintessential Impeachable Offense 6

    B.   The House Has Proven that President Trump Corruptly Pressured Ukraine to
    Interfere in the Presidential Election for His Personal Benefit 13

II.   PRESIDENT TRUMP MUST BE REMOVED FOR OBSTRUCTING CONGRESS 20

    A.   President Trump's Claim of Transparency Ignores the Facts 21

    B.   President Trump Categorically Refused to Comply with the House's Impeachment
    Inquiry 22

    C.   President Trump's Assertion of Invented Immunities Does Not Excuse His
    Categorical Obstruction 23

III. THE HOUSE CONDUCTED A CONSTITUTIONALLY VALID IMPEACHMENT PROCESS 25

    A.   The Constitution Does Not Authorize President Trump to Second Guess the
    House's Exercise of Its "Sole Power of Impeachment" 26

    B.   President Trump Received Fair Process 29

INTRODUCTION

President Trump's brief confirms that his misconduct is indefensible. To obtain a personal political "favor" designed to weaken a political rival, President Trump corruptly pressured the newly elected Ukrainian President into announcing two sham investigations. As leverage against Ukraine in his corrupt scheme, President Trump illegally withheld hundreds of millions of dollars in security assistance critical to Ukraine's defense against Russian aggression, as well as a vital Oval Office meeting. When he got caught, President Trump sought to cover up his scheme by ordering his Administration to disclose no information to the House of Representatives in its impeachment investigation. President Trump's efforts to hide his misdeeds continue to this day, as do his efforts to solicit foreign interference. President Trump must be removed from office now because he is trying to cheat his way to victory in the 2020 Presidential election, and thereby undermine the very foundation of our democratic system.

President Trump's lengthy brief to the Senate is heavy on rhetoric and procedural grievances, but entirely lacks a legitimate defense of his misconduct. It is clear from his response that President Trump would rather discuss anything other than what he actually did. Indeed, the first 80 pages of his brief do not meaningfully attempt to defend his conduct—because there is no defense for a President who seeks foreign election interference to retain power and then attempts to cover it up by obstructing a Congressional inquiry. The Senate should swiftly reject President Trump's bluster and evasion, which amount to the frightening assertion that he may commit whatever misconduct he wishes, at whatever cost to the Nation, and then hide his actions from the representatives of the American people without repercussion.

First, President Trump's argument that abuse of power is not an impeachable offense is wrong—and dangerous. That argument would mean that, even accepting that the House's recitation of the facts is correct—which it is—the House lacks authority to remove a President who sells out our democracy and national security in exchange for a personal political favor. The Framers of our Constitution took pains to ensure that such egregious abuses of power would be impeachable. They specifically rejected a proposal to limit impeachable offenses to treason and bribery and included the term "other high Crimes and Misdemeanors."[1]

There can be no reasonable dispute that the Framers would have considered a President's solicitation of a foreign country's election interference in exchange for critical American military and diplomatic support to be an impeachable offense. Nor can there be any dispute that the Framers would have recognized that allowing a President to prevent Congress from investigating his misconduct would nullify the House's "sole Power of Impeachment."[2] No amount of legal rhetoric can hide the fact that President Trump exemplifies why the Framers included the impeachment mechanism in the Constitution: to save the American people from these kinds of threats to our republic.

Second, President Trump's assertion that impeachable offenses must involve criminal conduct is refuted by two centuries of precedent and, if accepted, would have intolerable consequences. But this argument has not been accepted in previous impeachment proceedings and should not be accepted here. As one member of President Trump's legal team previously conceded, President Trump's theory would mean that the President could not be impeached even if he allowed an enemy power to invade and conquer American territory.[3] The absurdity of that argument demonstrates why every serious constitutional scholar to consider it—including the House Republicans' own legal

---

[1] U.S. Const., Art. II, § 4.
[2] U.S. Const., Art. I, § 2, cl. 5.
[3] *See* Alan Dershowitz, *The Case Against Impeaching Trump* 26-27 (2018).

expert—has rejected it.[4] The Framers intentionally did not tie "high Crimes and Misdemeanors" to the federal criminal code—which did not exist at the time of the Founding—but instead created impeachment to cover severe abuses of the public trust like those of President Trump.

Third, President Trump now claims that he had virtuous reasons for withholding from our ally Ukraine sorely needed security assistance and that there was no actual threat or reward as part of his proposed corrupt bargain. But the President's after-the-fact justifications for his illegal hold on security assistance cannot fool anybody. The reason President Trump jeopardized U.S. national security and the integrity of our elections is even more pernicious: he wanted leverage over Ukraine to obtain a personal, political favor that he hoped would bolster his reelection bid.

If withholding the security assistance to Ukraine had been a legitimate foreign policy act, then there is no reason President Trump's staff would have gone to such lengths to hide it, and no reason President Trump would have tried so hard to deny the obvious when it came to light. It is common sense that innocent people do not behave like President Trump did here. As his own Acting Chief of Staff Mick Mulvaney bluntly confessed and as numerous other witnesses confirmed, there was indeed a quid pro quo with Ukraine. The Trump Administration's message to the American people was clear: "We do that all the time with foreign policy."[5] Instead of embracing what his Acting Chief of Staff honestly disclosed, President Trump has tried to hide what the evidence plainly reveals: the Emperor has no clothes.

Fourth, President Trump's assertion that he has acted with "transparency" during this impeachment is yet another falsehood. In fact, unlike any of his predecessors, President Trump

---

[4] *See, e.g.*, Jonathan Turley, Written Statement, *The Impeachment Inquiry into President Donald J. Trump: The "Constitutional Basis" for Presidential Impeachment* 10-11 (Dec. 4, 2019), https://perma.cc/92PY-MBVY; Charlie Savage, *'Constitutional Nonsense': Trump's Impeachment Defense Defies Legal Consensus*, N.Y. Times (Jan. 20, 2020), https://perma.cc/76TD-94XT.
[5] Statement of Material Facts ¶ 121 (Jan. 18, 2020) (Statement of Facts) (filed as an attachment to the House's Trial Memorandum).

categorically refused to provide the House with *any* information and demanded that the entire Executive Branch coverup his misconduct. President Trump's subordinates fell in line.

Similarly wrong is the argument by President Trump's lawyers that his blanket claim of immunity from investigation should now be understood as a valid assertion of executive privilege—a privilege he never actually invoked. And President Trump's continued attempt to justify his obstruction by citing to constitutional separation of powers misunderstands the nature of an impeachment. His across-the-board refusal to provide Congress with information and his assertion that his own lawyers are the sole judges of Presidential privilege undermines the constitutional authority of the people's representatives and shifts power to an imperial President.

Fifth, President Trump's complaints about the House's impeachment procedures are meritless excuses. President Trump was offered an eminently fair process by the House and he will receive additional process during the Senate proceedings, which, unlike the House investigation, constitute an actual trial. As President Trump recognizes, the Senate must "decide for itself all matters of law and fact."[6]

The House provided President Trump with process that was just as substantial—if not more so—than the process afforded other Presidents who have been subject to an impeachment inquiry, including the right to call witnesses and present evidence. Because he had too much to hide, President Trump did not take advantage of what the House offered him and instead decided to shout from the sidelines—only to claim that the process he obstructed was unfair. President Trump's lengthy trial brief does not explain why, even now, he has not offered any documents or witnesses in his defense or provided any information in response to the House's repeated requests. This is not how an innocent person behaves. President Trump's process arguments are simply part

---

[6] Trial Memorandum of President Donald J. Trump at 13 (Jan. 20, 2020) (Opp.).

of his attempt to cover up his wrongdoing and to undermine the House in the exercise of its constitutional duty.

Finally, President Trump's impeachment trial is an effort to *safeguard* our elections, not override them. His unsupported contentions to the contrary have it exactly backwards. President Trump has shown that he will use the immense powers of his office to manipulate the upcoming election to his own advantage. Respect for the integrity of this Nation's democratic process requires that President Trump be removed before he can corrupt the very election that would hold him accountable to the American people.

In addition, President Trump is wrong to suggest that the impeachment trial is an attempt to overturn the prior election. If the Senate convicts and removes President Trump from office, then the Vice President elected by the American people in 2016 will become the President.[7] The logic of President Trump's argument is that because he was elected once and stands for reelection again, he cannot be impeached no matter how egregiously he betrays his oath of office. This type of argument would not have fooled the Framers of our Constitution, who included impeachment as a check on Presidents who would abuse their office for personal gain, like President Trump.

*   *   *

The Framers anticipated that a President might one day seek to place his own personal and political interests above those of our Nation, and they understood that foreign interference in our elections was one of the gravest threats to our democracy. The Framers also knew that periodic democratic elections cannot serve as an effective check on a President who seeks to manipulate the

---

[7] As the then-House Managers explained in President Clinton's impeachment trial, "[t]he 25th Amendment to the Constitution ensures that impeachment and removal of a President would not overturn an election because it is the elected Vice President who would replace the President not the losing presidential candidate." Reply of the U.S. House of Representatives to the Trial Mem. of President Clinton, *in Proceedings of the United States Senate in the Impeachment Trial of President Willian Jefferson Clinton, Volume II: Floor Trial Proceedings*, S. Doc. No. 106-4, at 1001 (1999).

those elections. The ultimate check on Presidential misconduct was provided by the Framers through the power to impeach and remove a President—a power that the Framers vested in the representatives of the American people.

Indeed, on the eve of his impeachment trial, President Trump continues to insist that he has done nothing wrong. President Trump's view that he cannot be held accountable, except in an election he seeks to fix in his favor, underscores the need for the Senate to exercise its solemn constitutional duty to remove President Trump from office. If the Senate does not convict and remove President Trump, he will have succeeded in placing himself above the law. Each Senator should set aside partisanship and politics and hold President Trump accountable to protect our national security and democracy.

ARGUMENT

I. PRESIDENT TRUMP MUST BE REMOVED FOR ABUSING HIS POWER

A. President Trump's Abuse of Power Is a Quintessential Impeachable Offense

President Trump contends that he can abuse his power with impunity—in his words, "do whatever I want as President"[8]—provided he does not technically violate a statute in the process. That argument is both wrong and remarkable. History, precedent, and the words of the Framers conclusively establish that serious abuses of power—offenses, like President Trump's, that threaten our democratic system—are impeachable.

President Trump's own misconduct illustrates the implications of his position. In President Trump's view, as long as he does not violate a specific statute, then the only check on his corrupt abuse of his office for his personal gain is the need to face reelection—even if the very goal of his abusive behavior is to cheat in that election. If President Trump were to succeed in his scheme and

---

[8] Statement of Facts ¶ 164.

6

win a second and final term, he would face no check on his conduct. The Senate should reject that dangerous position.

1. *The Framers Intended Impeachment as a Remedy for Abuse of High Office.* President Trump appears to reluctantly concede that the fear that Presidents would abuse their power was among the key reasons that the Framers adopted an impeachment remedy.[9] But he contends that abuse of power was never intended to be an impeachable offense in its own right.[10]

President Trump's focus on the label to be applied to his conduct distracts from the fundamental point: His conduct is impeachable whether it is called an "abuse of power" or something else. The Senate is not engaged in an abstract debate about how to categorize the particular acts at issue; the question instead is whether President Trump's conduct is impeachable because it is a serious threat to our republic. For the reasons set forth in the House Manager's opening brief, the answer is plainly yes.

In any event, President Trump is wrong that abuses of power are not impeachable. The Framers focused on the toxic combination of corruption and foreign interference—what George Washington in his Farewell Address called "one of the most baneful foes of republican government."[11] James Madison put it simply: The President "might betray his trust to foreign powers."[12]

To the Framers, such an abuse of power was the quintessential impeachable conduct. They therefore rejected a proposal to limit impeachable offenses to only treason and bribery. They recognized the peril of setting a rigid standard for impeachment, and adopted terminology that

---

[9] Opp. at 57 n.383.
[10] Opp. at 1-2.
[11] George Washington, Farewell Address (Sept. 19, 1796), *George Washington Papers, Series 2, Letterbooks 1754-1799: Letterbook 24, April 3, 1793 – March 3, 1797*, Library of Congress.
[12] 2 *The Records of the Federal Convention of 1787*, at 66 (Max Farrand ed., 1911).

would encompass what George Mason termed the many "great and dangerous offenses" that might

"subvert the Constitution."[13] The Framers considered and rejected as too narrow the word

"corruption," deciding instead on the term "high Crimes and Misdemeanors" because it would

encompass the type of "abuse or violation of some public trust"—the abuse of power—that

President Trump committed here.[14]

2. *Impeachable Conduct Need Not Violate Established Law.* President Trump argues that a

President's conduct is impeachable only if it violates a "known offense defined in existing law."[15]

That contention conflicts with constitutional text, Congressional precedents, and the overwhelming

consensus of constitutional scholars.

The Framers borrowed the term "high Crimes and Misdemeanors" from British practice and

state constitutions. As that term was applied in England, officials had long been impeached for non-

statutory offenses, such as the failure to spend money allocated by Parliament, disobeying an order

of Parliament, and appointing unfit subordinates.[16] The British understood impeachable offenses to

be "so various in their character, and so indefinable in their actual involutions, that it is almost

impossible to provide systematically for them by positive law."[17]

---

[13] *Id.* at 550.

[14] *The Federalist No. 65* (Alexander Hamilton); *see The Federalist Nos. 68* (Alexander Hamilton); *The Federalist No. 69* (Alexander Hamilton).

[15] Opp. at 14-16.

[16] Raoul Berger, *Impeachment: The Constitutional Problems* 67-69 (1973).

[17] 2 Joseph Story, Commentaries on the Constitution of the United States § 762 (1833). The President's brief selectively quotes Blackstone's *Commentaries* for the proposition that impeachment in Britain required a violation of "known and established law." Opp. at 15. But that reflected the well-known and established nature of the parliamentary impeachment process, not some requirement that the underlying conduct violate a then-existing law. *See also* 4 William Blackstone, *Commentaries on the Law of England* *5 n.7 (1836) ("The word *crime* has no technical meaning in the law of England. It seems, when it has a reference to positive law, to comprehend those acts which subject the offender to punishment. When the words *high crimes and misdemeanors* are used in prosecutions by impeachment, the words *high crimes* have no definite signification, but are used merely to give greater solemnity to the charge.").

American precedent confirms that the Impeachment Clause is not confined to a statutory code. The articles of impeachment against President Nixon turned on his abuse of power, rather than on his commission of a statutory offense. Many of the specific allegations set forth in those three articles did not involve any crimes. Instead, the House Judiciary Committee emphasized that President Nixon's conduct was "undertaken for his own personal political advantage and not in furtherance of any valid national policy objective"[18]—and *expressly* stated that his abuses of power warranted removal regardless whether they violated a specific statute.[19]

Previous impeachments were in accord. In 1912, for example, Judge Archibald was impeached and convicted for using his position to generate business deals with potential litigants in his court, even though this behavior had not been shown to violate any then-existing statute or laws regulating judges. The House Manager in the Archibald impeachment asserted that "[t]he decisions of the Senate of the United States, of the various State tribunals which have jurisdiction over impeachment cases, and of the Parliament of England all agree that an offense, in order to be impeachable, need not be indictable either at common law or under any statute."[20] As early as 1803, Judge Pickering was impeached and then removed from office by the Senate for refusing to allow an appeal, declining to hear witnesses, and appearing on the bench while intoxicated and thereby "degrading … the honor and dignity of the United States."[21]

---

[18] *Impeachment of Richard M. Nixon, President of the United States: Report of the Comm. on the Judiciary, H. of Representatives*, H. Rep. No. 93-1305, at 139 (1974).

[19] *See id.* at 136.

[20] *Proceedings of the U.S. Senate and the House of Representatives in the Trial of Impeachment of Robert W. Archbald*, Vol. II, S. Doc. No. 62-1140, at 1399 (1913).

[21] *Extracts from the Journal of the U.S. Senate in All Cases of Impeachment Presented by the House of Representatives, 1798-1904*, S. Doc. No. 62-876, at 20-22 (1912).

9

President Trump's argument conflicts with a long history of scholarly consensus, including among "some of the most distinguished members of the [Constitutional] convention."[22] As a leading early treatise on the Constitution explained, impeachable offenses "are not necessarily offences against the general laws … [for] [i]t is often found that offences of a very serious nature by high officers are not offences against the criminal code, but consist in abuses or betrayals of trust, or inexcusable neglects of duty."[23] In his influential 1833 treatise, Supreme Court Justice Joseph Story similarly explained that impeachment encompasses "misdeeds … as peculiarly injure the commonwealth by the abuse of high offices of trust," whether or not those misdeeds violate existing statutes intended for other circumstances.[24] Story observed that the focus was not "crimes of a strictly legal character," but instead "what are aptly termed, political offences, growing out of personal misconduct, or gross neglect, or usurpation, or habitual disregard of the public interests, in the discharge of the duties of political office."[25]

The fact that impeachment is not limited to violations of "established law" reflects its basic function as a remedy reserved for office-holders who occupy special positions of trust and power. Statutes of general applicability do not address the ways in which those to whom impeachment applies may abuse their unique positions. Limiting impeachment only to those statutes would defeat its basic purpose.

Modern constitutional scholars overwhelmingly agree. That includes one of President Trump's own attorneys, who argued during President Clinton's impeachment: "It certainly doesn't have to be a crime, if you have somebody who completely corrupts the office of president, and who

---

[22] S. Doc. No. 62-1140, at 1401 (1913) (citing 15 *The American and English Encyclopedia of Law* 1066 (John Houston Merrill ed., 1891)).

[23] *See* Thomas M. Cooley, *The General Principles of Constitutional Law* 159 (1880).

[24] 2 Story § 788.

[25] *Id.* § 762.

abuses trust and who poses great danger to our liberty."[26] More recently, that attorney changed

positions and now maintains that a President cannot be impeached even for allowing a foreign

sovereign to conquer an American State.[27] The absurdity of that argument helps explain why it has

been so uniformly rejected.

Even if President Trump were correct that the Impeachment Clause covers only conduct

that violates established law, his argument would fail. President Trump concedes that "high crimes

and misdemeanors" encompasses conduct that is akin to the terms that precede it in the

Constitution—treason and bribery.[28] And there can be no reasonable dispute that his misconduct is

closely akin to bribery. "The corrupt exercise of power in exchange for a personal benefit defines

impeachable bribery."[29] Here, President Trump conditioned his performance of a required duty

(disbursement of Congressionally appropriated aid funds to Ukraine) on the receipt of a personal

benefit (the announcement of investigations designed to skew the upcoming election in his favor).

This conduct carries all the essential qualities of bribery under common law and early American

precedents familiar to the Framers.[30] It would be all the more wrong in their view because it

involves a solicitation to a foreign government to manipulate our democratic process. And

---

[26] James Walker, *Alan Dershowitz Said a "Technical Crime" Wasn't Needed for Impeachment in Resurfaced 1998 Interview*, Newsweek (Jan. 20, 2020), https://perma.cc/6JCG-2GDW (*Dershowitz 1998 Interview*).

[27] Dershowtiz at 26-27.

[28] Opp. at 14.

[29] *Impeachment of Donald J. Trump, President of the United States: Report of the Comm. on the Judiciary of the H. of Representatives, together with Dissenting Views, to Accompany H. Res. 755*, H. Rep. No. 116-346, at 42 n. 207 (2019) (quotation marks omitted); *see* 2 Story § 794. Notably, President Trump's counsel, Professor Dershowitz, indicated in a recent television appearance that he and Professor Tribe agree on this point. *See Dershowitz 1998 Interview*, https://perma.cc/6JCG-2GDW.

[30] *See, e.g., Gilmore v. Lewis*, 12 Ohio 281, 286 (1843) (For "public officers, ... [i]t is an indictable offence, in them, to exact and receive any thing, but what the law allows, for the performance of their legal duties," because "at common law, being against sound policy, and, *quasi*, extortion."); *accord Kick v. Merry*, 23 Mo. 72, 75 (1856); *United States v. Matthews*, 173 U.S. 381, 384-85 (1899) (collecting cases).

11

President Trump did actually violate an "established law": the Impoundment Control Act.[31] Thus, even under his own standard, President Trump's conduct is impeachable.

3. *Corrupt Intent May Render Conduct an Impeachable Abuse of Power.* President Trump next contends that the Impeachment Clause does not encompass any abuse of power that turns on the President's reasons for acting. Thus, according to President Trump, if he could perform an act for legitimate reasons, then he necessarily could perform the same act for corrupt reasons.[32] That argument is obviously wrong.

The Impeachment Clause itself forecloses President Trump's argument. The specific offenses enumerated in that Clause—bribery and treason—both turn on the subjective intent of the actor. Treason requires a "disloyal mind" and bribery requires corrupt intent.[33] Thus, a President may form a military alliance with a foreign nation because he believes that doing so is in the Nation's strategic interests, but if the President forms that same alliance for the purpose of taking up arms and overthrowing the Congress, his conduct is treasonous. Bribery turns on similar considerations of corrupt intent. And, contrary to President Trump's assertion, past impeachments have concerned "permissible conduct that had been simply done with the wrong subjective motives."[34] The first and second articles of impeachment against President Nixon, for example, charged him with using the powers of his office with the impermissible goals of obstructing justice and targeting his political opponents—in other words, for exercising Presidential power based on impermissible reasons.[35]

---

[31] *Matter of Office of Mgmt. & Budget—Withholding of Ukraine Sec. Assistance*, B-331564 (Comp. Gen. Jan. 16, 2020), https://perma.cc/5CDX-XLX6.

[32] Opp. at 28.

[33] *Cramer v. United States*, 325 U.S. 1, 30-31 (1945) (Treason); *United States v. Sun-Diamond Growers of California*, 526 U.S. 398, 404-05 (1999) (Bribery).

[34] Opp. at 30.

[35] *See* H. Rep. No. 93-1305 (1974).

12

There are many acts that a President has "objective" authority to perform that would constitute grave abuses of power if done for corrupt reasons. A President may issue a pardon because the applicant demonstrates remorse and meets the standards for clemency, but if a President issued a pardon in order to prevent a witness from testifying against him, or in exchange for campaign donations, or for other corrupt motives, his conduct would be impeachable—as our Supreme Court unanimously recognized nearly a century ago.[36] The same principle applies here.

B. The House Has Proven that President Trump Corruptly Pressured Ukraine to Interfere in the Presidential Election for His Personal Benefit

President Trump withheld hundreds of millions of dollars in military aid and an important Oval Office meeting from Ukraine, a vulnerable American ally, in a scheme to extort the Ukrainian government into announcing investigations that would help President Trump and smear a potential rival in the upcoming U.S. Presidential election. He has not come close to justifying that misconduct.

1. President Trump principally maintains that he did not in fact condition the military aid and Oval Office meeting on Ukraine's announcement of the investigations—repeatedly asserting that there was "no quid pro quo."[37] The overwhelming weight of the evidence refutes that assertion. And President Trump has effectively muzzled witnesses who could shed additional light on the facts.

Although President Trump argues that he "did not make any connection between the assistance and any investigation,"[38] his own Acting Chief of Staff, Mick Mulvaney, admitted the opposite during a press conference—conceding that the investigation into Ukrainian election

---

[36] *Ex Parte Grossman*, 267 U.S. 87, 122 (1925) (the President could be impeached for using his pardon power in a manner that destroys the Judiciary's power to enforce its orders).
[37] Statement of Facts ¶ 114.
[38] Opp. at 81.

13

interference was part of "why we held up the money."[39] After a reporter inquired about this

concession of a quid pro quo, Mr. Mulvaney replied, "[W]e do that all the time with foreign policy,"

added, "get over it," and then refused to explain these statements by testifying in response to a

House subpoena.[40] The President's brief does not even address Mr. Mulvaney's admission.

Ambassador Taylor also acknowledged the quid pro quo, stating, "I think it's crazy to withhold

security assistance for help with a political campaign."[41] And Ambassador Sondland testified that

the existence of a quid pro quo regarding the security assistance was as clear as "two plus two equals

four."[42] President Trump's lawyers also avoid responding to these statements.

The same is true of the long-sought Oval Office meeting. As Ambassador Sondland

testified: "I know that members of this committee frequently frame these complicated issues in the

form of a simple question: Was there a quid pro quo?" He answered that, "with regard to the

requested White House call and the White House meeting, the answer is yes."[43] Ambassador Taylor

reaffirmed the existence of a quid pro quo regarding the Oval Office meeting, testifying that "the

meeting President Zelensky wanted was conditioned on the investigations of Burisma and alleged

Ukrainian interference in the 2016 U.S. elections."[44] Other witnesses testified similarly.[45]

---

[39] Statement of Facts ¶ 121.

[40] Id.

[41] Id. ¶ 118.

[42] Id. ¶ 101.

[43] Id. ¶ 52.

[44] Transcript, *Impeachment Inquiry: Ambassador William B. Taylor and George Kent: Hearing Before the H. Permanent Select Comm. on Intelligence*, 116th Cong. 35 (Nov. 13, 2019) (statement of Ambassador Taylor).

[45] Transcript, *Impeachment Inquiry: Fiona Hill and David Holmes: Hearing Before the H. Permanent Select Comm. on Intelligence*, 116th Cong. 18-19 (Nov. 21, 2019) (statement of Mr. Holmes) ("[I]t was made clear that some action on Burisma/Biden investigation was a precondition for an Oval Office visit.").

President Trump's principal answer to this evidence is to point to two conversations in which he declared to Ambassador Sondland and Senator Ron Johnson that there was "no quid pro quo."[46] Both conversations occurred after the President had been informed of the whistleblower complaint against him, at which point he obviously had a strong motive to come up with seemingly innocent cover stories for his misconduct.

In addition, President Trump's brief omits the second half of what he told Ambassador Sondland during their call. Immediately after declaring that there was "no quid pro quo," the President insisted that "President Zelensky must announce the opening of the investigations and he should want to do it."[47] President Trump thus conveyed that President Zelensky "must" announce the sham investigations in exchange for American support—the very definition of a quid pro quo, notwithstanding President Trump's self-serving, false statement to the contrary. Indeed that statement shows his consciousness of guilt.

President Trump also asserts that there cannot have been a quid pro quo because President Zelensky and other Ukrainian officials have denied that President Trump acted improperly.[48] But the evidence shows that Ukrainian officials understood that they were being used "as a pawn in a U.S. reelection campaign."[49] It is hardly surprising that President Zelensky has publicly denied the existence of a quid pro quo given that Ukraine remains critically dependent on continued U.S. military and diplomatic support, and given that President Zelensky accordingly has a powerful incentive to avoid angering an already troubled President Trump.

---

[46] *See* Opp. at 87-88.
[47] Statement of Facts ¶ 114.
[48] Opp. at 84-85.
[49] Statement of Facts ¶ 68.

President Trump's assertion that the evidence of a quid pro quo cannot be trusted because it is "hearsay" is incorrect.[50] The White House's readout of the July 25 phone call itself establishes that President Trump linked military assistance on President Zelensky's willingness to do him a "favor"—which President Trump made clear was to investigate former Vice President Biden and alleged Ukrainian election interference.[51] One of the people who spoke directly to President Trump—and whose testimony therefore was not hearsay—was Ambassador Sondland, who confirmed the existence of a quid pro quo and provided some of the most damning testimony against President Trump.[52] Other witnesses provided compelling corroborating evidence of the President's scheme.[53]

President Trump's denials of the quid pro quo are, therefore, plainly false. There is a term for this type of self-serving denial in criminal cases—a "false exculpatory"—which is strong evidence of guilt.[54] When a defendant "intentionally offers an explanation, or makes some statement tending to show his innocence, and this explanation or statement is later shown to be false," such a false statement tends to show the defendant's consciousness of guilt.[55] President Trump's denial of the quid pro quo underscores that he knows his scheme to procure the sham investigations was improper, and that he is now lying to cover it up.

---

[50] Opp. at 87.
[51] Statement of Facts ¶¶ 75-80.
[52] *See, e.g., id.* ¶ 52.
[53] *See, e.g., id.* ¶¶ 49-67.
[54] *See, e.g., United States v. Kahan*, 415 U.S. 239, 240-41 (1974) (per curiam).
[55] *United States v. Penn*, 974 F.2d 1026, 1029 (8th Cir. 1992).

2. President Trump next argues that he withheld urgently needed support for Ukraine for reasons unrelated to his political interest.[56] But President Trump's asserted reasons for withholding the military aid and Oval Office meeting are implausible on their face.[57]

President Trump never attempted to justify the decision to withhold the military aid and Oval Office meeting on foreign policy grounds when it was underway. To the contrary, President Trump's lawyer Rudy Giuliani acknowledged about his Ukraine work that "this isn't foreign policy."[58] President Trump sought to hide the scheme from the public and refused to give any explanation for it even within the U.S. government. He persisted in the scheme after his own Defense Department warned—correctly—that withholding military aid appropriated by Congress would violate federal law, and after his National Security Advisor likened the arrangement to a "drug deal."[59] And he released the military aid shortly after Congress announced an investigation[60]—in other words, after he got caught. The various explanations that President Trump now presses are after-the-fact pretexts that cannot be reconciled with his actual conduct.[61]

The Anti-Corruption Pretext. The evidence shows that President Trump was actually indifferent to corruption in Ukraine before Vice President Biden became a candidate for President.

---

[56] Opp. at 89.

[57] As the Supreme Court reiterated in rejecting a different pretextual Trump Administration scheme, when reviewing the Executive's conduct, it is not appropriate "to exhibit a naiveté from which ordinary citizens are free." *Dep't of Commerce v. New York*, 139 S. Ct. 2551, 2575 (2019) (quoting *United States v. Stanchich*, 550 F.2d 1294, 1300 (2d Cir. 1977) (Friendly, J.)).

[58] Statement of Facts ¶ 18. President Trump's brief never addresses the role of Mr. Giuliani, who served as President Trump's principal agent in seeking an announcement of the investigations.

[59] *Id.* ¶ 59.

[60] *Id.* ¶ 131.

[61] After Congress began investigating President Trump's conduct, the White House Counsel's Office reportedly conducted an internal review of "hundreds of documents," which "reveal[ed] extensive efforts to generate an after-the-fact justification" for the hold ordered by President Trump. Josh Dawsey et al., *White House Review Turns Up Emails Showing Extensive Effort to Justify Trump's Decision to Block Ukraine Military Aid*, Wash. Post (Nov. 24, 2019), https://perma.cc/99TX-5KFE. These documents would be highly relevant in this Senate trial.

17

After Biden's candidacy was announced, President Trump remained uninterested in anti-corruption measures in Ukraine beyond announcements of two sham investigations that would help him personally.[62] In fact, he praised a corrupt prosecutor and recalled a U.S. Ambassador known for her anti-corruption efforts. President Trump did not seek *investigations* into alleged corruption—as one would expect if anti-corruption were his goal—but instead sought only *announcements* of investigations—because those announcements are what would help him politically.

As Ambassador Sondland testified, President Trump "did not give a [expletive] about Ukraine," and instead cared only about "big stuff" that benefitted him personally like "the Biden investigation."[63] While President Trump asserts that he released the aid in response to Ukraine's actual progress on corruption,[64] in fact he released the aid two days after Congress announced an investigation into his misconduct. And President Trump's claim that the removal of the former Ukrainian prosecutor general encouraged him to release the aid is astonishing.[65] On the July 25 call with President Zelensky, President Trump praised that very same prosecutor—and Mr. Giuliani continues to meet with that prosecutor to try to dig up dirt on Vice President Biden to this day.[66]

The Burden-Sharing Pretext. Until his scheme was exposed, President Trump never attempted to attribute his hold on military aid to a concern about other countries not sharing the burden of supporting Ukraine.[67] One reason he never attempted to justify the hold on these grounds is that it is not grounded in reality. Other countries in fact contribute substantially to Ukraine. Since 2014, the European Union and European financial institutions have committed over $16 billion to Ukraine.[68]

---

[62] *See* Statement of Facts ¶ 88.
[63] *Id.* ¶ 88.
[64] Opp. at 94-95.
[65] Opp. at 94.
[66] Statement of Facts ¶¶ 81, 144-45.
[67] *See id.* ¶¶ 41-48.
[68] *See id.* ¶¶ 30-32.

In addition, President Trump *never even asked* European countries to increase their contributions to Ukraine as a condition for releasing the assistance. He released the assistance even though European countries did not change their contributions. President Trump's asserted concern about burden-sharing is impossible to credit given that he kept his own Administration in the dark about the issue for months, never made any contemporaneous public statements about it, never asked Europe to increase its contribution,[69] and released the aid without any change in Europe's contribution only two days after an investigation into his scheme commenced.[70]

The Burisma Pretext. The conspiracy theory regarding Vice President Biden and Burisma is baseless. There is no credible evidence to support the allegation that Vice President Biden encouraged Ukraine to remove one of its prosecutors in an improper effort to protect his son. To the contrary, Biden was carrying out official U.S. policy—with bipartisan support—when he sought that prosecutor's ouster because the prosecutor was known to be corrupt.[71] In any event, the prosecutor's removal made it *more likely* that Ukraine would investigate Burisma, not less likely—a fact that President Trump does not attempt to dispute. The allegations against Biden are based on events that occurred in late 2015 and early 2016—yet President Trump only began to push Ukraine to investigate these allegations in 2019, when it appeared likely that Vice President Biden would enter the 2020 Presidential race to challenge President Trump's reelection.

The Ukrainian-Election-Interference Pretext. The Intelligence Community, Senate Select Committee on Intelligence, and Special Counsel Mueller all unanimously found that Russia—not Ukraine—interfered in the 2016 election. President Trump's own FBI Director confirmed that American law enforcement has "no information that indicates that Ukraine interfered with the 2016

---

[69] *See id.*
[70] *See id.* ¶ 131.
[71] *Id.*

presidential election."[72] In fact, the theory of Ukrainian interference is Russian propaganda—"a fictional narrative that is being perpetrated and propagated by the Russian security services themselves" to drive a wedge between the United States and Ukraine.[73]

Thanks to President Trump, this Russian propaganda effort is spreading. In November, President Vladimir Putin said, "Thank God no one is accusing us of interfering in the U.S. elections anymore; now they're accusing Ukraine."[74] President Trump is correct in asserting "that the United States has a 'compelling interest … in limiting the participation of foreign citizens in activities of American democratic self-government'"[75]—and that is exactly why his misconduct is so harmful, and warrants removal from Office.

II.   PRESIDENT TRUMP MUST BE REMOVED FOR OBSTRUCTING CONGRESS

President Trump has answered the House's constitutional mandate to enforce its "sole power of Impeachment"[76] with open defiance: obstructing this constitutional process wholesale by withholding documents, directing witnesses not to appear, threatening those who did, and declaring both the courts and Congress powerless to compel his compliance. As President Trump flatly stated, "I have an Article II, where I have the right to do whatever I want as president."[77] President Trump now seeks to excuse his obstruction by falsely claiming that he has been transparent and by hiding behind hypothetical executive privilege claims that he has never invoked and that do not apply.

---

[72] *Id.* ¶ 13.

[73] *Id.* ¶ 14.

[74] *'Thank God': Putin thrilled U.S. 'political battles' over Ukraine taking focus off Russia*, Associated Press (Nov. 20, 2019), https://perma.cc/7ZHY-44CY.

[75] Opp. at 100.

[76] U.S. Const., Art. I, § 2, cl. 5.

[77] Statement of Facts ¶ 164.

20

A.   President Trump's Claim of Transparency Ignores the Facts

President Trump does not appear to dispute that obstructing Congress during an

impeachment investigation is itself an impeachable offense. He instead falsely insists that he "has

been extraordinarily transparent about his interactions with President Zelensky[]."[78]

President Trump's transparency claim bears no resemblance to the facts. In no uncertain

terms, President Trump has stated that "we're fighting all the subpoenas [from Congress]."[79] Later,

through his White House Counsel, President Trump directed the entire Executive Branch to defy

the House's subpoenas for documents in the impeachment—and as a result not a single document

from the Executive Branch was produced to the House.[80] He also demanded that his current and

former aides refuse to testify—and as a result nine Administration officials under subpoena refused

to appear.[81] That is a cover-up, and there is nothing transparent about it.

President Trump emphasizes that he publicly released the memorandum of the July 25 call

with President Zelensky. But President Trump did so only after the public had already learned that

he had put a hold on military aid to Ukraine and after the existence of the Intelligence Community

whistleblower complaint became public.[82] The fact that President Trump selectively released limited

information under public pressure, only to obstruct the House's investigation into his corrupt

scheme, does not support his assertion of transparency.

---

[78] Opp. at 35.

[79] Statement of Facts ¶ 164.

[80] *Id.* ¶¶ 179-83.

[81] *Id.* ¶¶ 186-87.

[82] *See* Michael D. Shear & Maggie Haberman, *Do Us a Favor": Call Shows Trump's Interest in Using U.S. Power for His Gain*, N.Y. Times (Sept. 25, 2019), https://perma.cc/B7P9-BPK2; Karoun Demirjian et al., *Trump Ordered Hold on Military Aid Days Before Calling Ukrainian President, Officials Say*, Wash. Post (Sept. 23, 2019), https://perma.cc/N7PQ-K9WB; Letter from Michael K. Atkinson, Inspector Gen. of the Intelligence Community, to Chairman Adam Schiff, House Permanent Select Comm. on Intelligence, and Ranking Member Devin Nunes, House Permanent Select Comm. on Intelligence (Sept. 9, 2019), https://perma.cc/K78N-SMRR.

B. President Trump Categorically Refused to Comply with the House's Impeachment Inquiry

In an impeachment investigation, the House has a constitutional entitlement to information concerning the President's misconduct. President Trump's categorical obstruction would, if accepted, seriously impair the impeachment process the Framers carefully crafted to guard against Presidential misconduct.[83]

President Trump asserts that individualized disputes regarding responses to Congressional subpoenas do not rise to the level of an impeachable offense.[84] But this argument distorts the categorical nature of his refusal to comply with the House's impeachment investigation. President Trump has refused *any and all* cooperation and ordered his Administration to do the same. No President in our history has so flagrantly undermined the impeachment process.

President Nixon ordered "[a]ll members of the White House Staff [to] appear voluntarily when requested by the committee," to "testify under oath," and to "answer fully all proper questions."[85] Even so, the Judiciary Committee voted to impeach him for not *fully* complying with House subpoenas when he withheld complete responses to certain subpoenas on executive privilege grounds. The Committee emphasized that "the doctrine of separation of powers cannot justify the withholding of information from an impeachment inquiry" because "the very purpose of such an inquiry is to permit the [House], acting on behalf of the people, to curb the excesses of another branch, in this instance the Executive."[86] If President Nixon's obstruction of Congress raised a

---

[83] *See The Federalist No. 69* (Alexander Hamilton).

[84] Opp. at 48-54.

[85] Remarks by President Nixon (Apr. 17, 1973), *reprinted in Statement of Information: Hearings Before the Comm. on the Judiciary, H. of Representatives: Book IV—Part 2, Events Following the Watergate Break-in* (1974).

[86] H. Rep. No. 93-1305, at 208 (1974).

"slippery slope" concern, then President Trump's complete defiance takes us to the "bottom of the slope, surveying the damage to our Constitution."[87]

President Trump's attempt to fault *the House* for not using "other tools at its disposal" to secure the withheld information—such as seeking judicial enforcement of its subpoenas[88]—is astonishingly disingenuous. President Trump cannot tell the House that it must litigate the validity of its subpoenas while simultaneously telling the courts that they are powerless to enforce them.[89]

C. President Trump's Assertion of Invented Immunities Does Not Excuse His Categorical Obstruction

Having used the power of his office to stonewall the House's impeachment inquiry, President Trump has now enlisted his lawyers in the White House Counsel's Office—and coopted his Department of Justice's Office of Legal Counsel—to justify the cover-up.[90] But his lawyers' attempts to excuse his obstruction do not work.

One fact is essential to recognize: President Trump *has never actually invoked executive privilege.* That is because, under longstanding law, invoking executive privilege would require President Trump to identify with particularity the documents or communications containing sensitive material

---

[87] H. Rep. No. 116-346, at 161. President Trump's new lawyer, Kenneth Starr similarly argued that President Clinton's assertion of executive privilege in grand jury proceedings, which "thereby delayed any potential congressional proceedings," constituted conduct "inconsistent with the President's Constitutional duty to faithfully execute the laws. *Communication from Kenneth W. Starr, Independent Counsel, Transmitting a Referral to the United States House of Representatives Filed in Conformity with the Requirements of Title 28, United States Code, Section 595(c)*, H. Doc. No. 105-310, at 129, 204 (1998).

[88] Opp. at 48-49 & n.336.

[89] *See* Statement of Facts ¶ 192; Def.'s Mot. to Dismiss, or in the Alternative, for Summ. J. at 20, *Kupperman v. U.S. House of Representatives*, No. 19-3224 (D.D.C. Nov. 14, 2019), ECF No. 40; Defs.' and Def.-Intervenors' Mot. to Dismiss at 46-47, *Comm. on Ways & Means v. U.S. Dep't of the Treasury*, No. 19-1974 (D.D.C. Sept. 6, 2019), ECF No. 44; *see also* Brief for Def.-Appellant at 2, 32-33, *Comm. on the Judiciary v. McGahn*, No. 19-5331 (D.C. Cir. Dec. 9, 2019).

[90] Opp. app'x C (*House Committees' Authority to Investigate for Impeachment*, 44 Op. O.L.C. (2020)) at 1-2, 37 (opining that the House's impeachment investigation was not authorized under the House's "sole Power of Impeachment," U.S. Const., Art. I, § 2, cl. 5).

that he seeks to protect. Executive privilege generally cannot be used to shield misconduct, and it does not apply here because President Trump and his associates have repeatedly and publicly discussed the same matters he claims must be kept secret.

President Trump instead maintains that his advisors should be "absolutely immune" from compelled Congressional testimony.[91] But this claim of absolute immunity—which turns on the theory that certain high-level Presidential advisors are "alter egos" of the President—cannot possibly justify the decision to withhold the testimony of the lower-level agency officials whom President Trump ordered not to testify. Regardless, the so-called absolute immunity theory is an invention of the Executive Branch, and every court to consider this argument has rejected it—including the Supreme Court in an important ruling requiring President Nixon to disclose the Watergate Tapes.[92] In other words, President Trump's defenses depend on arguments that disgraced former President Nixon litigated and lost.

President Trump additionally attempts to justify his obstruction on the ground that Executive Branch counsel were barred from attending House depositions.[93] Of course, the absence of counsel at depositions does not excuse the President's refusal to disclose documents in response to the House's subpoenas. And the decades-old rule excluding agency counsel from House depositions—first adopted by a Republican House of Representatives majority—exists for good reasons. It prevents agency officials implicated in Congressional investigations from misleadingly shaping the testimony of agency employees. It also protects the rights of witnesses to speak freely

---

[91] *See* Opp. at 43-44.

[92] *See United States v. Nixon*, 418 U.S. 683, 706 (1974) ("neither the doctrine of separation of powers, nor the need for confidentiality of high-level communications, without more, can sustain an absolute, unqualified Presidential privilege of immunity from judicial process").

[93] Opp. at 46-47.

and without fear of reprisal[94]—a protection indisputably necessary here given that President Trump has repeatedly sought to intimidate and silence witnesses against him.[95]

President Trump finally maintains that complying with the impeachment inquiry would somehow violate the constitutional separation of powers doctrine.[96] This argument is exactly backwards. The President cannot reserve the right to be the arbiter of his own privilege—particularly in an impeachment inquiry designed by the Framers of the Constitution to uncover Presidential misconduct. The fact that President Trump has found lawyers willing to concoct theories on which documents or testimony might be withheld is no basis for his refusal to comply with an impeachment inquiry. The check of impeachment would be little check at all if the law were otherwise.

III. THE HOUSE CONDUCTED A CONSTITUTIONALLY VALID IMPEACHMENT PROCESS

As explained in the House Managers' opening brief, the House conducted a full and fair impeachment proceeding with robust procedural protections for President Trump, which he tellingly chose to ignore. The Committees took 100 hours of deposition testimony from 17 witnesses with personal knowledge of key events, and all Members of the Committees as well as Republican and Democratic staff were permitted to attend and given equal opportunity to ask questions. The Committees heard an additional 30 hours of public testimony from 12 of those witnesses, including three requested by the Republicans.[97] President Trump's lawyers were invited to participate at the public hearings before the Judiciary Committee.[98] Rather than do so, he urged the House: "if you are going to impeach me, do it now, fast, so we can have a fair trial in the Senate."[99]

---

[94] *See* H. Rep. No. 116-346, at 544.

[95] *See, e.g.*, Statement of Facts ¶ 190.

[96] Opp. at 36; *see id.* at 48-54.

[97] *See* Statement of Facts ¶¶ 188-89; H. Rep. No. 116-346, at 130.

[98] Statement of Facts ¶ 176.

[99] H. Rep. No. 116-346, at 12 (quoting Letter from Pat A. Cipollone, Counsel to the President, to Jerrold Nadler, Chairman, H. Comm. on the Judiciary (Dec. 6, 2019)).

But faced with his Senate trial, President Trump now cites a host of procedural hurdles that he claims the House failed to satisfy. Nobody should be fooled by this obvious gamesmanship.

A. The Constitution Does Not Authorize President Trump to Second Guess the House's Exercise of Its "Sole Power of Impeachment"

President Trump's attack on the House's conduct of its impeachment proceedings disregards the text of the Constitution, which gives the House the "sole Power of Impeachment,"[100] and empowers it to "determine the Rules of its Proceedings."[101] As the Supreme Court has observed, "the word 'sole'"—which appears only twice in the Constitution—"is of considerable significance."[102] In the context of the Senate's "sole" power over impeachment trials, the Court stressed that this term means that authority is "reposed in the Senate and nowhere else"[103] and that the Senate "alone shall have authority to determine whether an individual should be acquitted or convicted."[104] The House's "sole Power of Impeachment" likewise vests it with the independent authority to structure its impeachment proceedings in the manner it deems appropriate. The Constitution leaves no room for President Trump to object to how the House, in the exercise of its "sole" power to determine impeachment, conducted its proceedings here.

President Trump has no basis to assert that the impeachment inquiry was "flawed from the start" because it began before a formal House vote was taken.[105] Neither the Constitution nor the House rules requires such a vote.[106] And notwithstanding President Trump's refrain that the

---

[100] U.S. Const., Art. I, § 2, cl. 5.
[101] U.S. Const., Art. I, § 5, cl. 2.
[102] *Nixon v. United States*, 506 U.S. 224, 230 (1993).
[103] *Id.* at 229.
[104] *Id.* at 231.
[105] Opp. at 4.
[106] One district court presented with this same argument recently concluded that "[i]n cases of presidential impeachment, a House resolution has never, in fact, been required to begin an impeachment inquiry," explaining that the argument "has no textual support in the U.S. Constitution [or] the governing rules of the House." *In re Application of Comm. on Judiciary, U.S. House of Representatives, for an Order Authorizing Release of Certain Grand Jury Materials*, No. 19-48 (BAH), 2019

26

House's inquiry "violated every precedent and every principle of fairness followed in impeachment inquiries for more than 150 years,"[107] House precedent makes clear that an impeachment inquiry does not require a House vote. As even President Trump is forced to acknowledge, several impeachment inquiries conducted in the House "did not begin with a House resolution authorizing an inquiry."[108] In fact, the House has *impeached* several federal judges without ever passing such a resolution[109]—and the Senate then convicted and removed them from office.[110] Here, by contrast, the House adopted a resolution confirming the investigating Committees' authority to conduct their inquiry into "whether sufficient grounds exist for the House of Representatives to exercise its Constitutional power to impeach Donald John Trump, President of the United States of America."[111]

President Trump is similarly mistaken that a formal "delegation of authority" to the Committees was needed at the outset.[112] The House adopted its Rules[113]—"a power that the Rulemaking Clause [of the Constitution] reserves to each House alone"[114]—but did not specify rules that would govern impeachment inquiries. It is thus difficult to understand how the House's

---

WL 5485221, at *27 (D.D.C. Oct. 25, 2019). Although both President Trump and the Office of Legal Counsel of the Department of Justice go to great lengths to criticize the district court's analysis, *see, e.g.*, Opp. app'x C at 38 n.261, the Department of Justice tellingly has declined to advance these arguments in litigation on the appeal of this decision.

[107] Opp. at 1.

[108] Opp. at 41.

[109] *See In re Application of Comm. on Judiciary*, 2019 WL 5485221, at *26 (citing proceedings relating to Judges Walter Nixon, Alcee Hastings, and Harry Claiborne).

[110] *See Proceedings in the United States Senate in the Impeachment Trial of Walter Nixon, Jr., a Judge of the United States District Court for the Southern District of Mississippi*, S. Doc. No. 101-22, at 439 (1989); *Proceedings of the United States Senate in the Impeachment Trial of Alcee L. Hastings, a Judge of the United States District Court for the Southern District of Florida*, S. Doc. No. 101-18, at 705 (1989); *Proceedings of the United States Senate in the Impeachment Trial of Harry E. Claiborne, a Judge of the United States District Court for the District of Nevada*, S. Doc. No. 99-48, at 298 (1986).

[111] H. Res. 660, 116th Cong. (2019); Statement of Facts ¶ 162.

[112] *See* Opp. at 37-38.

[113] *See* H. Res. 6, 116th Cong. (2019).

[114] *Barker v. Conroy*, 921 F.3d 1118, 1130 (D.C. Cir. 2019) (quotation marks omitted).

impeachment inquiry could violate its rules or delegation authority. Not only did Speaker Pelosi instruct the Committees to proceed with an "impeachment inquiry,"[115] but in passing H. Res. 660, the full House "directed" the Committees to "continue their ongoing investigations as part of the existing House of Representatives inquiry" into impeachment.[116]

President Trump is wrong that the subpoenas were "unauthorized and invalid" because they were not approved in advance by the House.[117] There is no requirement in either the Constitution or the House Rules that the House vote on subpoenas. Indeed, such a requirement would be inconsistent with the operations of the House, which in modern times largely functions through its Committees.[118] The absence of specific procedures prescribing how the House and its Committees must conduct impeachment inquiries allows those extraordinary inquiries to be conducted in the manner the House deems most fair, efficient, and appropriate. But even assuming a House vote on the subpoenas was necessary, there was such a vote here. When it adopted H. Res. 660, the House understood that numerous subpoenas had already been issued as part of the impeachment inquiry. As the Report accompanying the Resolution explained, these "duly authorized subpoenas" issued to the Executive Branch "remain in full force."[119]

---

[115] Statement of Facts ¶ 161.

[116] *Id.* ¶ 162; *see* H. Res. 660.

[117] Opp. at 37; *see* Opp. at 41.

[118] *See, e.g.*, House Rule XI.1(b)(1) (authorizing standing committees of the House to "conduct at any time such investigations and studies as [they] consider[] necessary or appropriate"); *see also id.* X1.2(m)(1)(B) (authorizing committees to "require, by subpoena or otherwise, the attendance and testimony of such witnesses and the production of such books, records, correspondence, memoranda, papers, and documents as [they] consider[] necessary").

[119] *Directing Certain Committees to Continue Their Ongoing Investigations as Part of the Existing House of Representatives Inquiry into Whether Sufficient Grounds Exist for the House of Representatives to Exercise its Constitutional Power to Impeach Donald John Trump, President of the United States of America, and for Other Purposes*, H. Rep. No. 116-266, at 3 (2019).

B.   President Trump Received Fair Process

As his lawyers well know, the various criminal trial rights that President Trump demands have no place in the House's impeachment process.[120] It is not a trial, much less a criminal trial to which Fifth or Sixth Amendment guarantees would attach. The rights President Trump has demanded have never been recognized in any prior Presidential impeachment investigation, just as they have never been recognized for a person under investigation by a grand jury—a more apt analogy to the House's proceedings here.

Although President Trump faults the House for not allowing him to participate in depositions and witness interviews, no President has ever been permitted to participate during this initial fact-finding process. For example, the Judiciary Committee during the Nixon impeachment found "[n]o record ... of any impeachment inquiry in which the official under investigation participated in the investigation stage preceding commencement of Committee hearings."[121] In both the President Nixon and President Clinton impeachment inquiries, the President's counsel was not permitted to participate in or even attend depositions and interviews of witnesses.[122] And in both cases, the House relied substantially on investigative findings by special prosecutors and grand juries, neither of which allowed the participation of the target of the investigation.[123] Indeed, the reasons grand jury proceedings are kept confidential—"to prevent subornation of perjury or tampering with the witnesses who may testify before grand jury" and "encourage free and untrammeled disclosures

---

[120] Opp. at 57.

[121] H. Rep. No. 116-346, at 19 (quoting Impeachment Inquiry Staff, H. Comm. on the Judiciary, *Memorandum: Presentation Procedures for the Impeachment Inquiry* 11, 93d Cong. (1974)).

[122] *Id.* at 19, 21.

[123] *See id.* at 17-22.

by persons who have information,"[124]—apply with special force here, given President Trump's chilling pattern of witness intimidation.[125]

In his litany of process complaints, President Trump notably omits the fact that his counsel could have participated in the proceedings before the Judiciary Committee in multiple ways. The President, through his counsel, could have objected during witness examinations, cross-examined witnesses, and submitted evidence of his own.[126] President Trump simply chose not to have his counsel do so. Having deliberately chosen not to avail himself of these procedural protections, President Trump cannot now pretend they did not exist.

Nor is the President entitled to have the charges against him proven beyond a reasonable doubt.[127] That burden of proof is applicable in criminal trials, where lives and liberties are at stake, not in impeachments. For this reason, the Senate has rejected the proof-beyond-a-reasonable-doubt standard in prior impeachments[128] and instead has "left the choice of the applicable standard of proof to each individual Senator."[129] Once again, President Trump's lawyers well know this fact.

President Trump's contention that the Articles of Impeachment must fail on grounds of "duplicity" is wrong. President Trump alleges that the Articles are "structurally deficient" because they "charge[] multiple different acts as possible grounds for sustaining a conviction."[130] But this simply repeats the argument from the impeachment trial of President Clinton, which differed from President Trump's impeachment in this critical respect. Where the articles charged President

---

[124] *United States v. Procter & Gamble Co.*, 356 U.S. 677, 681 n.6 (1958).

[125] Statement of Facts ¶¶ 177, 190.

[126] Statement of Facts ¶ 163; 165 Cong. Rec. E1357 (2019) (Impeachment Inquiry Procedures in the Committee on the Judiciary Pursuant to H. Res. 660); *see id.* at (A)(3), (B)(2)–(3), (C)(1)–(2), (4).

[127] Opp. at 20-21.

[128] *See, e.g.*, 132 Cong. Rec. S29124-94 (daily ed. October 7, 1986).

[129] Cong. Research Serv., 98-990 A, *Standard of Proof in Senate Impeachment Proceedings* 6 (1999), https://perma.cc/9YKG-TJLH.

[130] Opp. at 107-09.

Clinton with engaging in "one or more" of several acts,[131] the Articles of Impeachment against President Trump do not. This difference distinguishes President Trump's case from President Clinton's—where, in any event, the Senate rejected the effort to have the articles of impeachment dismissed as duplicitous. The bottom line is that the House knew precisely what it was doing when it drafted and adopted the Articles of Impeachment against President Trump, and deliberately avoided the possible problem raised in the impeachment proceedings against President Clinton.

*　　*　　*

There was no procedural flaw in the House's impeachment inquiry. But even assuming there were, that would be irrelevant to the *Senate's* separate exercise of its "sole Power to try all Impeachments."[132] Any imagined defect in the House's previous proceedings could be cured when the evidence is presented to the Senate at trial. President Trump, after all, touted his desire to "have a fair trial in the Senate."[133] And as President Trump admits, it is the Senate's "constitutional duty to decide for itself all matters of law and fact bearing upon this trial."[134] Acquitting President Trump on baseless objections to the House's process would be an abdication by the Senate of this duty.

---

[131] H. Res. 611, 105th Cong. (1998).

[132] U.S. Const., Art. I, § 3, cl. 6. *See also Nixon v. United States*, 506 U.S. 224, 229-31 (1993).

[133] H. Rep. No. 116-346, at 12 (quoting Letter from Pat A. Cipollone, Counsel to the President, to Jerrold Nadler, Chairman, H. Comm. on the Judiciary (Dec. 6, 2019)).

[134] Opp. at 13.

Respectfully submitted,

United States House of Representatives

Adam B. Schiff
Jerrold Nadler
Zoe Lofgren
Hakeem S. Jeffries
Val Butler Demings
Jason Crow
Sylvia R. Garcia

January 21, 2020   *U.S. House of Representatives Managers**

---

* The House Managers wish to acknowledge the assistance of the following individuals in preparing this reply memorandum: Douglas N. Letter, Megan Barbero, Josephine Morse, Adam A. Grogg, William E. Havemann, Jonathan B. Schwartz, Christine L. Coogle, Lily Hsu, and Nate King of the House Office of General Counsel; Daniel Noble, Daniel S. Goldman, and Maher Bitar of the House Permanent Select Committee on Intelligence; Norman L. Eisen, Barry H. Berke, Joshua Matz, and Sophia Brill of the House Committee on the Judiciary; the investigative staff of the House Committee on Oversight and Reform; and David A. O'Neil, Anna A. Moody, David Sarratt, Laura E. O'Neill, and Elizabeth Nielsen.

32

www.ingramcontent.com/pod-product-compliance
Lightning Source LLC
Chambersburg PA
CDIIW000624030426
42336CB00018B/3070